S0-AEA-804

Guide to

Vermont's Day Hikes

Guide to
Vermont's Day Hikes

Jared Gange

Huntington Graphics
Burlington, Vermont

Sixth edition, June 2011
Copyright 2011, Huntington Graphics
All rights reserved
Printed in Canada

Gange, Jared
     Guide to Vermont's Day Hikes
     Includes index.
     ISBN 978-1-886064-41-6

Previous title: "Hiker's Guide to the Mountains of Vermont"

Graphic design & maps: John Hadden, Resting Lion Studio

UVM Student Intern: Emily Allen Ford

Please read before using this book:

   Hiking, like many outdoor endeavors, is a potentially dangerous activity. Participants in these activities assume responsibility for their actions and safety. No guide book can replace good judgment on the part of the user. Obtain the necessary skills and inform yourself about potential dangers before taking part in outdoor recreation activities. Neither the author nor publisher, nor anyone associated with this book, has any responsibility or liability for anyone who uses the information contained herein or who participates in the sport of hiking. Hike difficulty ratings, time estimates, or impressions are subjective and will vary from hiker to hiker depending on such things as ability, experience, confidence, or physical fitness. As a result, the author cannot assure the accuracy of the information in this book, including hike descriptions, maps, and directions. These may be unintentionally misleading or incorrect.

   Also note that access to hiking areas may be changed or revoked at any time. Hikers must be aware that publication of this book does not grant them permission nor a right to use the land on which the hikes mentioned in this book are located. Please obey posted signs that indicate a change in ownership or status of a trail or activity area.

Photo facing page: Summit Ridge of Mt. Mansfield by Jared Gange
Cover photo: Lars Gange
Back cover photos: Jim Fredericks, Jared Gange, John Hadden, Virginia Loughran

Guide to
Vermont's Day Hikes

- The 100 best day hikes
- All the major summits
- Guide to backcountry skiing

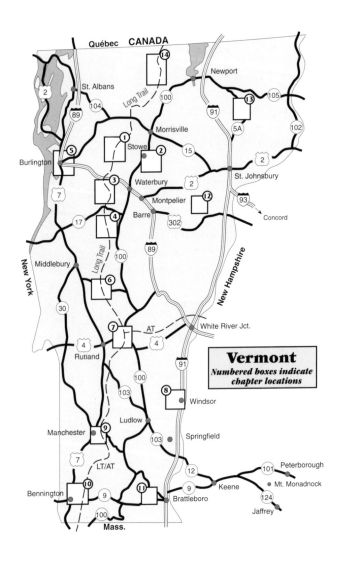

Québec **CANADA**

Newport

St. Albans

14

Long Trail

100

(104)

(89)

(2)

13

91

(105)

Morrisville

5A

(102)

1

Stowe

2

15

(2)

St. Johnsbury

5

Burlington

3

Waterbury

(2)

(7)

Montpelier

12

93

Barre

302

Concord

4

(17)

(89)

Long Trail

100

Middlebury

6

(30)

New York

7

AT

White River Jct.

(4)

Rutland

4

91

100

103

8

Windsor

Manchester

9

Ludlow

103

Springfield

(7)

LT/AT

12

101

Peterborough

10

9

11

9

Keene

Mt. Monadnock

Bennington

Brattleboro

124

100

Jaffrey

New Hampshire

Mass.

Vermont
Numbered boxes indicate
chapter locations

Contents

Introduction

The hundreds of miles of trails that wind through the mountains of Vermont — the Green Mountain State — have been enjoyed by hikers for many years. The terrain varies from gentle paths through hardwood forests to steep, rocky scrambles leading to breezy summits. We have tried to make this guide book easy to use by basing the chapters around familiar towns and mountains and presenting the popular hikes for these areas. The detailed maps that accompany the route descriptions show the hiking terrain and the driving approaches to the trailheads. Beginning with the Mount Mansfield region — our most important hiking area — we present the most commonly done hikes from the Camel's Hump, Worcester Range, Mad River Valley, Middlebury, Killington, Manchester, Bennington, Mount Snow, Brattleboro-Putney, Mount Ascutney, Groton State Forest, Northeast Kingdom, and Jay Peak areas. A brief introduction to mountains just across the border in Québec is provided, along with several important hikes in neighboring New Hampshire and Massachusetts.

Our focus here is on mountain hikes, that is, climbing up mountains, usually to the top, but always to a view or something of interest, such as a pond or a cabin. Rather than providing a list of all hiking trails in the state, or an arbitrary selection of hikes, our goal here is to offer the hiker a comprehensive, authoritative selection of hikes throughout Vermont.

In Vermont, hiking information traditionally has revolved around the Long Trail, the "footpath in the wilderness", which runs from the Massachusetts border, north to the Canadian border. Because of this traditional focus on the

Long Trail, the Green Mountain Club's early guide books concentrated on the Long Trail. Later the Green Mountain Club brought out a second guide book addressing the other trails in the state, i.e. trails not connected to the Long Trail. Since the vast majority of hiking today is day hiking, and since the day hikes turn out to be both on the Long Trail (Mount Mansfield, Camel's Hump, Mount Abraham, for example) and off the Long Trail (Mount Hunger, Stowe Pinnacle, Mount Ascutney, Mount Pisgah, for example), there would seem to be a need for a guide book that treats the day hikes of Vermont in a comprehensive, easy-to-use fashion. The *Guide to Vermont's Day Hikes* fills that need: It covers the classic hikes, the highest mountains—by most routes—and local favorites.

Hikers often give themselves long term, or long distance, hiking goals. This usually takes one of two forms: hiking the entire length of a trail, such as the Appalachian Trail, or climbing all the mountains on an established list, such as the 48 mountains over 4,000' in New Hampshire, the traditional 46 peaks in New York's Adirondacks over 4,000', or, most ambitiously, all 4,000' summits (114) in the Northeast. While long-distance hiking might be regarded by some as unimaginative drudgery, and peak-bagging an arbitrary pursuit, both goals are great motivators and encourage us to go places and experience things we otherwise would not. Here in Vermont, the best-known hiking goal is the 272-mile Long Trail. Most hikers do it section by section, usually taking a number of years to complete the entire trail. The *Guide to Vermont's Day Hikes* provides another option for a hiking goal: Do all 100 hikes in this book and you will have truly hiked Vermont!

Hiking times and distances

In the mountains, it is *walking time* rather than distance travelled that can give us a reliable measure of the actual effort needed to do a particular hike. A three-mile hike in gentle terrain obviously is going to take much less effort than a three-mile hike up Camel's Hump, which requires almost 2,000' of climbing. In the hike descriptions provided, round trip time, round trip distance, and approximate elevation gained are provided, with the time given first. Actual times will vary a great deal from hiker to hiker, or from day to day depending on trail (and hiker) condition. The times provided are determined partly by observation and partly by applying the standard formula of 2 miles per hour plus one half hour per 1,000' gain in elevation. Most hikers should find these time estimates reasonable: some will find them too low, some too high. By providing a *consistent* time rating, hikers using this guide should eventually be able to reliably plan the amount of time they will need for a given hike.

When travelling in the mountains, especially on longer, more ambitious hikes, the main comment about time has to be: Allow extra! It is up to you to build flexibility into your schedule so your group has the leeway to deal with any unplanned events or delays.

In some areas, trails are showing signs of overuse, and in other areas fragile vegetation is at risk. Please respect any signs—trail detours or requests not to walk off the trail, for example—that you might encounter. In fact, during the spring mud season, about mid-April to Memorial Day, many of the trails are closed. This is because of the much greater damage done by boots when trails are soft and muddy.

Getting started

Most of the routes in this book will be enjoyable for hikers of all levels of experience, and most can be done at a reasonable pace in a half day or less. Round trip times and distances are given for each hike, and difficult trail sections are noted. To get started, begin with the shorter hikes in your area. Find out what sort of footwear works for you and get an idea of how *your* normal hiking pace compares with the times given here. You probably already have done some form of hiking or extended walking, and the role of this guide is to enable you to discover Vermont's popular hikes. For those not comfortable with the do-it-yourself approach, there are organized hiking trips; these are noted in local newspapers. Here in Vermont, the Green Mountain Club (GMC) is the primary hiking organization. If you are a regular user of hiking trails, consider joining or supporting the GMC or your local hiking club. The Green Mountain Club has over a dozen local chapters, making the Club accessible throughout the state.

Hiking Guidelines

- Pick a route that is within your group's ability.
- Allow yourself plenty of time.
- Let someone know your plan, then stick to it.
- Exercise extra caution if hiking alone.
- Pack out what you pack in.
- Pets should be controlled at all times: on a leash near water sources and on summits above tree line.
- Take water/drinks with you. The Giardia parasite is widespread, so it is best to play it safe.
- Respect owner signs and private property.

Always take extra clothing: preferably something that will keep you dry *and* protect you from wind. Before starting out, remember there is always the possibility that the weather will deteriorate during your trip. Be prepared for this! The variability of weather is especially a concern for early summer and fall hikes, as even on fine days, the summits are cooler and breezier than the valleys below.

There is great variation in hiking abilities and tastes, and this in turn makes it difficult to give general advice on clothing and equipment. Work out what footwear works best for you by trying different options and by consulting your nearest outdoor outfitter. A number of Vermont's hiking and backpacking suppliers are represented in this guide. This recognizes the essential role they play in advising and educating the public about appropriate and cost-effective footwear, packs, parkas, and accessories. But they are also a source of local hiking information and current trail conditions. Some of them have assisted with the selection of hikes for this guide book. They are presented in the "Sponsors" section.

Catching wind on Mansfield's Chin   Jared Gange

Maps

In addition to the map coverage provided by the USGS (United States Geological Survey), excellent topographic hiking maps are available from three other sources. The Green Mountain Club publishes five maps: the very popular Vermont's Long Trail, and Camel's Hump and the Monroe Skyline, Mt. Mansfield and the Worcester Range, Killington Area, and the Northeast Kingdom. Two excellent, large scale maps are published by Map Adventures: Northern Vermont Hiking and the Mad River Valley. Lastly, National Geographic (Trails Illustrated) has recently published two Vermont hiking/road maps, Green Mountain National Forest: South and Green Mountain National Forest: North. With the exception of the USGS maps, all of these maps are widely available in stores.

The Vermont Atlas and Gazetteer (DeLorme) is useful in navigating back roads and finding trailheads.

A leisurely ascent of Mount Elmore   J. Gange

Hiking With Children

Most of the shorter hikes in this book, and the beginning sections of some of the longer hikes, are suitable for children. Views, especially distant views, do not always hold much fascination for kids. Their interests are usually closer at hand: stream crossings, bridges, rocky scrambles, wild animals, a lake, or a mountain hut. Try to break your hike into short, manageable sections.

Some tips: Leave your own, more ambitious hiking goals at home; there will be plenty of time for the longer hikes later. The idea is to get some walking exercise and have fun! Start out with very short trips, and if the interest is there, go with it. Hikes that last three or four hours, even with a moderate amount of climbing, are well with the reach of motivated six- or seven-year olds. Bringing a same-aged friend along can be a great motivator. Take plenty of favorite snacks and drinks. Remember to walk at a pace that suits your child, and set goals that are appropriate for their abilities. Lastly, be prepared to change your well-laid plans in mid-hike if something more interesting comes along.

1 Mount Mansfield Region

As the highest mountain in Vermont, and the dominant landmark in the Burlington area, Mount Mansfield (4,395') naturally receives a great deal of attention from hikers. The Long Trail traverses its 2-mile, open summit ridge, and there are nine hiking routes up the mountain. A gondola and a toll road to the summit ridge make the upper mountain accessible to everyone. The following pages describe the main routes up Mount Mansfield, as well as some nearby hikes: Sterling Pond, Elephant's Head, and Whiteface Mountain. Two areas to the south of Mansfield, Nebraska Notch, and Bolton Valley, also are included in this chapter.

1 Long Trail route up Mount Mansfield

The popular route from the Stowe side follows the Long Trail south from Route 108. The trail climbs steadily and steeply through woods, reaching **Taft Lodge** (caretaker in summer) after 1.7 miles and about 1.5 hours. From here, the trail is rougher and steeper, breaking into the open about 10 minutes past Taft. The exciting final section to the summit is up steep rocks. Although it is not really difficult, use caution, especially if the rocks are wet. The 360-degree view from the summit is spectacular. Return by the same route, or, for a route more protected from the elements, continue south from the summit on the Long Trail (LT) for 0.2 mile and turn left on the **Profanity Trail**. It uses a steep gully to descend directly to Taft Lodge, returning you to the Long Trail.

The summit ridge of Mt. Mansfield resembles an elongated face in profile with the **Chin** as the summit.

5 hours and 4.7 miles round trip. Elevation gain: 2,800'
Approach: From Stowe, go west on Rt. 108 for 8.5 miles, passing the ski area entrances and park at the Long Trail crossing in Smugglers Notch.

Approaching the summit of Mt. Mansfield   Lars Gange

2 The Gondola and the Cliff Trail

A quick way up Mansfield is to ride the gondola, then hike the remaining 0.7 mile to the summit. The gondola ends a few hundred feet below the summit ridge, and once the summit ridge is reached, it is an easy walk to the top. The problem is getting to the ridge; the **Cliff Trail** is quite difficult in a few places and involves sections of *very* steep climbing up some large boulders. Head right (south) 150' from the gondola to access the Cliff Trail. Once on the ridge, head right (north) on the **Long Trail** for 15 minutes (0.4 mile) to the top. Note this trail junction for your return. For an easier and longer descent route, from the top, head down the Long Trail the way you came, but stay on the open summit ridge (1.4 miles) to the **Toll Road**. Then continue down the Toll Road and turn left onto the first ski run, the **Nosedive**. Follow this and other ski runs down the mountain, returning to the base station and completing the loop.

3-4 hours and 4 miles total. (Descend via ski trails.)

Approach: The base of the gondola is 7.5 miles from Route 100 in Stowe, on Route 108, in Smugglers Notch.

3 Hell Brook Trail

Perhaps the most continuously steep and rough trail in Vermont, Hell Brook is not recommended for beginners. However, many experienced hikers (and expert powder skiers) will want to do this challenging trail. Not advised for the descent, especially when wet! After its long and arduous climb, the trail breaks into the open upon reaching the summit ridge, about 1.3 miles from the road. (**Hell Brook Cut-off Trail** branches left to **Taft Lodge** at 0.9 mile.) Head left to reach the **Long Trail** and follow it to the summit—only 1.8 miles from the road. The recommended descent route is via the Long Trail and Taft Lodge, leaving you with an easy 0.9-mile road walk (left) back to Big Spring.

4 hours and 5 miles round trip. Elevation gain: 2,600'
Approach: From Stowe, drive up the Mountain Road past the ski resort to Big Spring on right, 9 miles from Stowe and VT 100. Hell Brook Trail is 150' up the road on the left.

4 The Toll Road up Mount Mansfield

Starting from the Toll House on the Mountain Road, 6 miles from Stowe, the gravel-surfaced Toll Road climbs to the summit ridge of Mount Mansfield in 4.5 miles. From here, it is an easy and spectacular 1.4-mile hike north along the Long Trail to the **Chin**, Mount Mansfield's summit. Most drive up the Toll Road, but it is open to hikers at no charge. Once on the summit ridge, hikers are reminded to stay on the actual trail (or rock outcroppings) as the fragile arctic-alpine vegetation is easily damaged by foot traffic. The **Nose** (4,062'), the mountain's southern summit, looms above the parking area, and a short hike (20 minutes) brings you to its top. There are excellent views of the summit ridge for many miles in all directions. Guide books and maps can be purchased at the **Summit Station**, located at the top of the Toll Road.

Vermont's steepest: Hell Brook Trail
Jared Gange

5 The Nose (4,062') via the Haselton Trail

Angling up to the left from the base of the gondola (same approach as hike #2), the Haselton Trail climbs at a pleasant angle, crossing several ski trails before merging with **Nosedive** (ski run) and ending on the **Toll Road** (at 1.6 miles) just below the Octagon restaurant. Follow the Toll Road (right) 0.5 mile to the **Summit House** on the summit ridge. From here it's possible to continue on the road and then to the top of Mansfield's impressive second summit.

3-4 hours, 4.6 miles total. Elevation gain: 2,500'

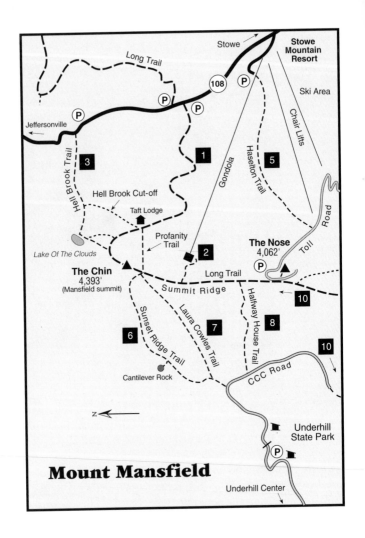

Mount Mansfield

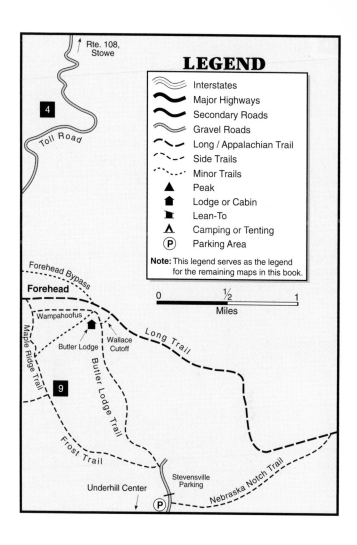

LEGEND

〜 Interstates
〜 Major Highways
〜 Secondary Roads
〜 Gravel Roads
- - Long / Appalachian Trail
- - - Side Trails
···· Minor Trails
▲ Peak
⬟ Lodge or Cabin
▮ Lean-To
⬭ Camping or Tenting
Ⓟ Parking Area

Note: This legend serves as the legend for the remaining maps in this book.

0 ½ 1
Miles

↑ Rte. 108, Stowe

4

Toll Road

Forehead Bypass

Forehead

Wampahoofus

Butler Lodge

Wallace Cutoff

Long Trail

Maple Ridge Trail

9

Butler Lodge Trail

Frost Trail

Stevensville Parking

Underhill Center

Nebraska Notch Trail

Sunset Ridge Trail

On the west side of Mount Mansfield, Sunset Ridge is the prominent ridge dropping off the summit. Because the ridge offers sweeping views of the Champlain Valley and the Adirondacks, this route is considered one of the finest hikes in Vermont — many would say *the* finest. Accordingly, it is often somewhat crowded, so you might want to get an early start on weekends. From **Underhill State Park** (nominal fee), ascend the moderate grades of the **CCC Road** for about a mile, where the Sunset Ridge Trail branches left. Continue on **Sunset Ridge Trail** as it climbs steeply through woods, eventually coming out on the broad, open ridge. From here to the **Chin** (the summit) the route is out in the open, and the grand westerly views of the Adirondacks and Lake Champlain are quite impressive, especially in late afternoon sun. The low-angle slabs make for easy but fun hiking.

Mt. Mansfield summit ridge, top of Sunset Ridge Trail   J. Gange

On the Forehead, Sunset Ridge in the background   J. Gange

On a hot summer day, make sure you have plenty to drink. Once on the summit ridge, bear left (north) on the **Long Trail** to the summit, 0.2 mile farther on. After enjoying the panoramic views, and the view of various ski lifts and runs on the other side of the mountain, descend by the route you came, carefully following signs.

5 hours and 6.6 miles round trip. Elevation gain: 2,550'
Approach: From Underhill (Route 15), drive to Underhill Center. Continue to Mountain Road, a short distance beyond and follow it to Underhill State Park.

Side trail: About 0.7 mile above the CCC Road, a short (0.1-mile) spur trail leads left to the well-known **Cantilever Rock**, a rock that juts about 25' out over the trail.

7 Laura Cowles Trail

From **Underhill State Park**, walk up the **CCC Road**. After about a mile, the Laura Cowles and Sunset Ridge trails branch left off the road. Then, after 0.1 mile, Laura Cowles Trail branches right. It ascends very directly to the summit ridge, at times climbing a rough stone stairway before rejoining the Sunset Ridge Trail just west of the Long Trail. The views on Laura Cowles are very limited until near the top. Take the Long Trail for the final 0.2 mile to the summit. The best descent route is via the open **Sunset Ridge**, thus you "walk into the view" as you hike down. This loop combination is a good variation on simply hiking up and down Sunset Ridge.

5 hours and 6 miles round trip. Elevation gain: 2,550'

8 Halfway House Trail

South of Laura Cowles, the Halfway House Trail also ascends Mansfield's west flank, but it offers better views than the Laura Cowles Trail. As for Laura Cowles and Sunset Ridge, start from **Underhill State Park** but continue on the CCC Road 0.2 mile past the Sunset Ridge turnoff. Here the Halfway House Trail branches off left and ascends to the summit ridge and the LT after 1.1 miles of very steep climbing. At the Long Trail, head left for 1.2 miles to the summit of Mansfield. The usual descent route would be via Sunset Ridge as this returns you to Underhill State Park. Thus this route is analogous to the Laura Cowles-Sunset Ridge loop, but it is somewhat longer.

5-6 hours and 6.8 miles round trip. Gain: 2,550'
Approach: From Underhill Center, drive to Underhill State Park. Start out as for Sunset Ridge.

The Laura Cowles Trail in winter   J. Gange

9 Maple Ridge

Sunset Ridge and Maple Ridge are the two main west ridges of Mount Mansfield. Maple Ridge descends from the Forehead (the southernmost summit) towards Underhill Center. From the parking area at the end of Stevensville Rd., take the **Frost Trail** to **Maple Ridge Trail**. Continue up the ridge to the **Forehead's** open summit at 3,940'. This route has some rather difficult sections—including a short cliff and a crevice jump—making it one of the most exciting trails in Vermont! The views constantly change as the trail works its way across huge slabs and around improbable rock formations. From the Forehead, either descend the way you came, follow the Long Trail (south/right), or continue (north/left on the LT) to the Nose (0.8 mi) or the Chin (1.7 mi). To descend south from the Forehead, follow the Long Trail right, passing over exciting, somewhat challenging terrain involving several ladders. Note: This route is not suitable for dogs. After 0.8 mile, branch right (Wallace Cut-off) to **Butler Lodge**. From here, continue down to Stevensville Rd. An easier descent option from the Forehead is to use the weather-protected Forehead Bypass, a pleasant route on much easier terrain through a cool and mossy birch wood. From the Forehead, head north on the LT 0.3 miles to pickup the Forehead Bypass. It rejoins the LT a few minutes before you reach the link to Butler Lodge. This hike is done in either direction.

5 hours and 5.5 miles round trip. Gain: 2,550'

Approach: From Underhill Center, drive to the end of Stevensville Road and park. Walk up the (gated) road, taking the Frost Trail (left) 0.2 mile from the car.

Maple Ridge-Forehead-Butler Lodge loop:
5 hours and 5 miles round trip. Gain: 2,550'

A steep section on Maple Ridge

Jared Gange

10 Maple Ridge - Sunset Ridge Loop

This is a fine, if rather vigorous, way to climb Mount Mansfield — call it the deluxe route from the west. From **Underhill State Park**, follow the gravel **CCC Road** about a mile to where the Sunset Ridge Trail branches off left. (There is a marked shortcut trail that cuts across the CCC Road several times and is an alternate route to this junction.) Bear right and continue along the road, which degrades into an unimproved track. The trail makes a gradual uphill climb while crossing several small brooks before coming to the **Maple Ridge Trail**. From the sign, the trail climbs steeply over smooth rocks before emerging onto Maple Ridge. The trail becomes increasingly steep in this section with several jumps and vertical climbs. (Great views now!) Upon reaching the **Forehead** of Mansfield, bear left on the **Long Trail** across several log puncheons before reaching a service road. The LT bears left on the road before re-entering the woods on the right and soon comes to the Mt. Mansfield Visitor Center. (An ascent of the **Nose** (4,062'), Mansfield's south summit, is recommended.) Continue along the spectacular, open **summit ridge** for about a mile and a half, eventually reaching the junction with the Sunset Ridge Trail. Here continue straight and make the short climb (0.3 mile) to the **Chin**, Mansfield's summit. From the summit, retrace your steps to the junction to pick up **Sunset Ridge Trail**. It descends the moderate slabs of Sunset Ridge: there ar huge views to the west. Below tree line, the trail descends steeply (it is slippery and rough in places) and then more moderately, passing a junction with the Cantilever Rock spur trail. From here it is a short descent to the CCC Rd. and Underhill State Park.

6 hours and 8 miles. Elevation gain: 2,950'

The Long Trail below the Forehead   Virginia Loughran

Sterling Pond   Matt Larson

11 Sterling Pond

This extremely popular hike leads to a pleasant mountain pond and, a short distance away, a sweeping view north from the top of a ski run. From **Smugglers Notch** (2,612'), take the well-maintained **Sterling Pond Trail** (formerly the Long Trail) north as it climbs fairly steeply and steadily. Bear left around the pond for a short distance to reach the ski area viewpoint. **Sterling Pond Shelter** is 0.3 mile farther on. Descend by the same route.

2 hours, 2.2 miles round trip. Elevation gain: 930'

Approach: Park at (the top of) Smugglers Notch on Route 108, 10 miles from Stowe and 8 miles from Jeffersonville.

12 Spruce Peak 3,380'

This moderate to steep climb on ski trails to the top of Spruce Peak leads to a cliff top overlook offering a dramatic view of nearby Mt. Mansfield directly across the chasm of Smugglers Notch. It is a great hike anytime outside of ski season, when you are obviously better off on skis. Basically the goal is to climb to the top of the Sensation Quad chairlift, and the most obvious route is the Sterling ski trail, to the right of the quad. At the top of the quad, continue straight up between the chairlift and the ski patrol building, then bear left, then right onto a narrower path, then left again, then right again. This zigzag maneuver should bring you to the rocky, precipitous perch high above Smugglers Notch. Relax and enjoy the view before descending.

2.5 hours and 3 miles roundtrip. Gain 1,750'

Approach: From Stowe take Route 108 (the Mountain Road) to Stowe Mountain Resort. Drive up to the resort hotel complex, but bear right and continue to the upper Spruce parking lot, about 0.8 mile from Route 108.

13 Long Trail Traverse of Mount Mansfield

The 10-mile traverse of the long ridge of our highest mountain from **Lake Mansfield** to **Smugglers Notch** is one of Vermont's most rugged and spectacular hikes. Sweeping views, an exciting 2 miles of trail above treeline, and some difficult climbs make this a memorable outing. The trip is done in either direction and with variations. To reach the trailhead for **Taylor Lodge**, drive to the end of Nebraska Valley from Stowe. Hike in past the Lake Mansfield Trout Club (private) and walk over easy terrain before climbing steeply to the lodge (space for 15) and the Long Trail at 1.6 miles. After avoiding **Nebraska Notch** proper (a jumble of huge boulders), the LT traverses the west flank of Dewey Mtn., passing **Twin Brooks tenting area** 2 miles from Taylor Lodge and reaching the side trail left to **Butler Lodge** 1.3 miles farther on. Butler (space for 14) is perched nicely, high on the mountain. Butler is a good overnight option. The next day return to the Long Trail and ascend the exposed slabs of the **Forehead** (use protected Forehead Bypass in bad weather). From the top of the Forehead, it is about 2 miles to the **Chin** (main summit), most of which is along the open summit ridge. Now walk the long, gentle summit ridge (a times rough and rocky) to the mountain's highest point. After enjoying the views, descend to **Taft Lodge** either via the somewhat exposed Long Trail (0.4 mile), or if the weather is bad, backtrack (0.2 mile) to the **Profanity Trail**, which drops (left) directly down to Taft. From the lodge down to Route 108, it is a pleasant 1.7 miles.

Distance: 10.7 miles, climbing: 4,000' Time: 1-2 days

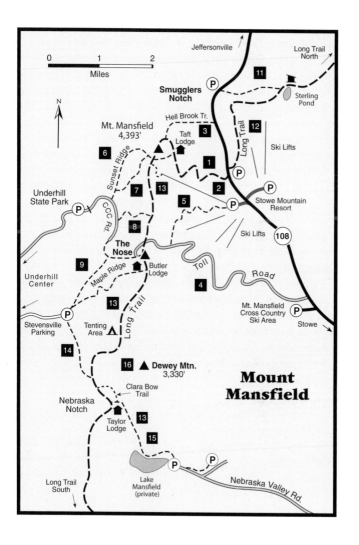

Mount Mansfield

14 Nebraska Notch from the west

From Stevensville parking, the Nebraska Notch Trail leads off to the right. After climbing gently through an open forest, the trail descends to cross a footbridge before making a brief climb to reach the **Long Trail** at 1.5 miles. Continue on the LT south (0.7 mile down past beaver ponds, then a steep climb) to **Taylor Lodge**, which is located just off the LT (left). The 0.4-mile **Clara Bow Trail** tackles the wild, boulder-filled ravine of Nebraska Notch proper and provides a fun, challenging loop variation to Taylor Lodge. To do this, head left 0.3 mile past the LT junction and thread your way past huge rocks, trees clinging to cliffs and through a cave-like grotto with a ladder exit. A beaver pond with commanding views of the notch appears on your left just before Taylor Lodge.

3 miles (1.5 to the LT, 2.2 to Taylor Lodge) and 2-3 hours round trip. Elevation gain: 520' (Same for the loop.)

Approach: From Underhill Center, take Pleasant Valley Road 0.2 miles north and turn east (right) on to Stevensville Road. Pass the winter parking area (on the left) and continue to the parking area at 2.8 miles.

Maps: *Northern Vermont Hiking (Map Adventures); Vermont's Long Trail (GMC); Recreation Map & Guide, Mt. Mansfield Region (Huntingtion Graphics)*

The beaver pond in Nebraska Notch   Matt Larson

15 Nebraska Notch (1,850') from the east

From Lake Mansfield Trout Club (private) at the end of the Nebraska Valley Road, follow the public hiking trail (Lake Mansfield Trail) through woods as it skirts along the north side of the lake. Then, after ascending a steep section and passing some small waterfalls, you reach Nebraska Notch, the **Long Trail** and **Taylor Lodge**. There are limited views of Nebraska Valley from the shelter. Return is by the same route. Northward from Taylor Lodge, the LT climbs, then descends sharply before commencing a fairly arduous ascent of Mount Mansfield via the Forehead, the Nose and the summit ridge. Southbound, the LT traverses Mounts Clark and Mayo before cresting 3,725-foot Bolton Mountain.

2.5 hours and 3 miles round trip. Gain: 750'

Approach: From Route 100, just south of Stowe, drive through Moscow to the hiker parking lot just below the Trout Club, at the upper end of Nebraska Valley.

16 Dewey Mountain 3,330'

There is no maintained trail up this steep, densely forested mountain. Seen from the east Dewey's sharp form is intriguing. Although not the shortest way, the route from the Mt. Mansfield Ski Touring Center is perhaps the easiest to describe. Following ski trails from the Ski Center, reach the Burt Trail (ski trail) and follow it to **Dewey Saddle** on Skytop Ridge. The upper section of the Burt offers a beautiful climb through old-growth forest with huge paper birches. From the small saddle, climb right, finding the best route you can. It should take you about 30 minutes to bushwhack to the heavily forested summit. Climb a tree to fully appreciate the excellent view! Return by the same route.

17 Whiteface Mountain 3,714'

The pointed summit of this steep-sided peak yields good views if you move through and around the trees. Whiteface also is referred to as Sterling Mountain, and the compact group of summits northeast of Smugglers Notch is known as the Sterling Range. From the car, walk in on a woods road for 2 miles (blue blazes) to where the **Whiteface Mountain Trail** turns off to the right. It climbs steadily, reaching **Whiteface Shelter** and the **Long Trail** after a mile (see map on page 163). Bear right 0.4 mile on the LT, which climbs steeply to the summit. Descend by the same route, or, for a good loop hike, continue south on the Long Trail past the Whiteface Trail junction, over **Morse Mountain**, past **Hagerman Lookout** to **Chilcoot Pass**, in the saddle below **Madonna Mountain** (This is Smugglers Notch Ski Area). From here, head left and descend extremely steeply 0.8 mile to **Beaver Meadow Lodge**. Keep left to return to the road used on the way in.

Vegetation Above the Tree Line

In Northern Vermont a phenomenon known as the tree line occurs at about 4,000' of elevation. Above this height, mainly because of lower average temperatures, trees do not thrive. While the transition from spruce-balsam forest to open mountainside can vary somewhat depending on the local "micro climate", it is quite abrupt when it does happen. Thus hikers can find themselves suddenly very exposed to the elements upon emerging from the protection of a dense forest onto a wind-blasted summit ridge. The brief transition zone is home to gnarled and wind-stunted trees called krummholz.

However, the above-treeline area is far from lifeless. A large variety of grasses, sedges, mosses, and flowers make their home in this "arctic-alpine" zone. The name is appropriate because our high mountain plants are also present in the sub-arctic latitudes of Labrador and Alaska. Some areas in the Northeast — the Alpine Garden on Mount Washington (New Hampshire), for example — are famous for their spring (June at this altitude) displays. Because the above-treeline areas in Vermont are extremely limited in size (a few summits), they receive a heavy concentration of hiker traffic. And because of the short growing season, and the plants' precarious existence generally, visitors must exercise extreme care not to step on or sit on any plants. Please leash your dogs and make sure everyone walks only on rock slabs or gravel areas.

Loop: 5 hours and 8.7 miles. Total elevation gain: 2,400'
Approach: From Morristown Corners (north of Stowe), head west on Walton Rd., then *south* on Cole Hill Rd. At 2 miles, turn right on Mud City Loop. At 4.4 miles, turn left on Beaver Meadow Rd. Park in the clearing at 5.8 miles.

18 Ricker Mountain 3,401'

From the ski area base lodge, ascend the ski slopes under or near the Vista Quad to the top of Vista Peak. From here, continue past the top of the lift and find the path that leads to the wooden observation tower. The views are excellent, especially of Camel's Hump. Descend by the same route.

2 hours and 2 miles round trip. Elevation gain: 1,400'

Approach: Drive to the Bolton Valley Ski Area. The 4-mile access road leaves Route 2 six miles west of Waterbury. From Burlington, use the I-89 Richmond exit and Route 2.

19 Bolton Mountain 3,725'

The isolated, rounded shape of this relatively high but viewless mountain is a prominent part of the landscape as seen from I-89 and Burlington. From Bolton's ski touring center, hike up the George's Gorge and Raven's Wind ski trails, eventually reaching the Long Trail. Continue (right) for about 0.7 mile to the top. Descend by the same route.

About 3.5 hours and 5 miles round trip. Elev. gain: 1,800'

20 Harrington's View 2,520'

For a shorter, and probably more interesting hike than the above, start from the Ski Touring Center and walk out Broadway to Bobcat. At the top of Bobcat, continue to Eagle's Nest, and from there, hike up to the Long Trail. Harrington's View, an open rock ledge with a nice view, is then about 20 minutes to the south (left). Return on the same trails.

2 hours, 3 miles, elevation gain: 500'

Approach: As above, drive to Bolton Valley Ski Area.

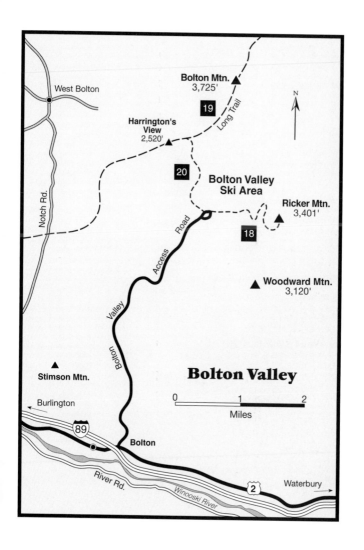

West Bolton

Bolton Mtn.
3,725'

19

Long Trail

Harrington's
View
2,520'

Notch Rd.

N

20

Bolton Valley
Ski Area

Ricker Mtn.
3,401'

Access Road

18

Woodward Mtn.
3,120'

Valley

Bolton

Stimson Mtn.

Bolton Valley

Burlington

0   1   2
Miles

89

Bolton

River Rd.

Winooski River

2

Waterbury

Just off the Long Trail, near Elephant's Head   J. Gange

Winter Activity on Mt. Mansfield

With a major ski area—Stowe Mountain Resort—occupying its eastern slopes, this is a busy mountain, winter and summer. And while the ski lifts do not quite reach the summit or the summit ridge, it is a relatively short climb from the Octagon (the high point of the ski lifts) along the Toll Road to the summit ridge. Once on the ridge, gentle terrain leads to the actual summit. From the summit ridge, backcountry skiers enjoy a number of options: the classic Teardrop Trail (see page 180) drops off the west (backside) of the mountain, ending in Underhill, and a number of difficult lines are available from the summit, including Hellbrook, an extremely steep hiking trail. Skiers can also traverse from the top of the gondola to reach Hellbrook and many other unofficial, off-piste runs.

For those with less inclination for very steep terrain, backcountry routes such as Overland Trail make for a great though still challenging outing. The trail climbs from Stevensville (Underhill) to the main ridge between Dewey and Mansfield before descending to the Mount Mansfield Ski Touring Center. An important variation on this tour is to continue (from the ridge) on the Underhill Trail, which eventually brings you to the Trapp Family cross country ski trail network. Here you can recharge your batteries (lunch, snacks) at the ski cabin.

In addition to the two cross country ski centers mentioned above, ski trips into Nebraska Notch (from Stevensville), Lake Mansfield (Nebraska Valley) and along the unplowed highway into Smugglers Notch are among the options for easier ski tours in the Mansfield region.

2 The Worcester Range

The impressive mountain wall that parallels Route 100 from Waterbury north past Stowe to Morrisville is known as the Worcester Range. High above Waterbury Center, the major hiking destination of the range, Mount Hunger is plainly visible—it is the bare, rounded knoll just to the right of a slightly higher point on the ridge. The Skyline Trail runs along this ridge from Mount Hunger north to Hogback Mountain and continues to Mount Worcester. Just north of Hogback Mtn., the trail forks with the left fork dropping steeply to merge with the Stowe Pinnacle Trail, which then leads down to Stowe Hollow. The right fork (Skyline Trail) continues north to Worcester Mountain.

21 Mount Hunger (south summit) 3,538'

This classic hike affords some of the best mountaintop views in Vermont: Camel's Hump looms to the southwest, Waterbury Reservoir is below, and Mt. Mansfield beckons to the northwest. The White Mountains of New Hampshire are visible on a clear day. From the parking area, the **Waterbury Trail** ascends through woods, gradually at first, then steadily and steeply in its upper section—at times clambering up giant "steps". The trail breaks into the open just below the top. Be sure to note your surroundings as you enter the open summit area in order to find *your* trail back. There are two other trails which depart from the summit. On a sunny summer day, relax and enjoy this hospitable mountain top. Mount Hunger is known for its blueberries.

4 hours, 3.8 miles round trip. Elev. gain: 2,290'

Approach: From Waterbury Center, just east of Route 100, drive north on Maple Street, then right on Loomis Hill Road. Stay left at 2.7 miles. Park at 3.7 miles.

Summit of Mt. Hunger Jared Gange

Just below the summit of Mount Hunger, on the Waterbury Trail, the trail to **White Rock Mountain** (3,194') branches right (sign). This rough trail leads to the interesting open rocks on White Rock Mountain, including a huge, level rock slab below the summit. The trail then heads around to the east side of the mountain and ends on the **Middlesex Trail** (the east side route up Mt. Hunger) about a mile from the top of Mount Hunger. Head left and make the steep, enjoyable climb to the summit. Then descend via the Waterbury Trail back to your starting point. This loop makes for an interesting variation if you are up for the extra hour or two of hiking.

22 Mount Hunger from Middlesex

Somewhat longer than the Waterbury route, the **Middlesex Trail** is the standard route from the Montpelier area. It is a more varied trail than the Waterbury route, and the upper section negotiates a series of interesting slabs. This route is not recommended when conditions are icy! The signage leaves something to be desired, but the blue-blazed trail is excellent and recommended as a change for those who usually climb Mount Hunger from the Waterbury side. At 1.5 miles, the **White Rock Trail** branches to the left (sign). Because there are two other trails off the top, note the route carefully as you approach the summit to avoid confusion on your descent. Mount Hunger's views are among the best. Camel's Hump, Mount Mansfield, Waterbury Reservoir, and the mountains of New Hampshire: All are in plain view.

4 hours and 5.6 miles round trip. Elevation gain: 1,900'
Approach: From Montpelier, drive north on Route 12 to Shady Rill Road and turn left. Proceed 2.2 miles, passing through one intersection and turning right on to Story Rd. at next intersection. At 2.6 miles, turn left onto Chase Rd., then left on N. Bear Swamp Rd. at 3.4 miles. Continue to large parking area (4.8 miles from Rt. 12).

23 Stowe Pinnacle   2,740'

A great hiking goal for families, the top of the Pinnacle has superb views and plenty of space for hikers to spread out and relax. This very popular, moderately strenuous hike starts out as a gentle climb (often somewhat muddy), before gradually getting steeper and rockier. The **Pinnacle Trail** levels off briefly in a saddle—a short spur trail leads left to a lookout over Stowe and Mt. Mansfield—then descends steeply a short distance before climbing to the dramatic

Relaxing on top of Stowe Pinnacle Jared Gange

open summit. Stay right at the (possibly unmarked) junction of the **Hogback Trail** (to Mount Hunger and Waterbury) about 0.2 mile below the top. From the rocky summit dome there is an unobstructed view of Stowe and its western wall of mountains. The view extends from Camel's Hump in the south to Jay Peak in the north, with the Worcester Range directly above. Descend by the same route. For a longer variation, see the Skyline Trail on page 47.

2.5-3 hours and 3 miles round trip. Gain: 1,520'
Approach: Take Goldbrook Road (1.5 miles south of Stowe on VT 100); at 0. 3 mile, turn left. At 1.8 miles turn right onto Upper Hollow Road and park on the left at 2.3 miles, in the marked hiker parking lot.

Maps: *Mt. Mansfield and the Worcester Range (GMC); Northern Vermont Hiking (Map Adventures); Recreation Map & Guide for Mount Mansfield Region (Huntington Graphics)*

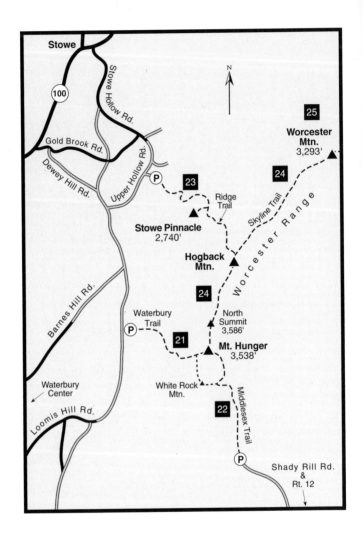

24 Skyline Trail

This relatively new and lightly used trail seems to be slowly gaining acceptance. To do the standard ridge traverse, climb Mount Hunger from the Waterbury Center side. (This is more convenient for car shuttling than from the Middlesex side.) From the south summit of **Mt. Hunger**, head left (north), and follow the blue-blazed trail as it works its way along the ridge, past the north summit of Hunger, to the top of Hogback Mountain (3,642'). Two tenths of a mile farther along, the **Hogback Trail/Ridge Trail** branches left off the Skyline Trail and descends steeply to the **Stowe Pinnacle Trail**. (This provides an option for a shorter version of the hike.) From this intersection with the Hogback Trail (now 3 miles north of Mt. Hunger), the Skyline Trail continues north for 6 miles to the summit of **Worcester Mtn.** (3,293'). From here it is 2.5 miles down the **Worcester Mountain Trail** to the village of Worcester on VT Route 12, north of Montpelier.

Skyline Trail only: Mt. Hunger-Worcester Mtn.:
5-6 hours and 9.2 miles, one way. Elev. gain: 2,000'

Waterbury trailhead to Worcester trailhead via Skyline Trail:
8-10 hours and 13.9 miles one way. Elev. gain: 4,500'

Approach: Same as for the trail up Mount Hunger from Waterbury Center, via Loomis Hill Road.

If you decide to descend via the Hogback Trail (see above) to the **Pinnacle Trail**, it is only a 0.2-mile detour (left and up) to the wide-open top of **Stowe Pinnacle** (dramatic views) and 1.3 miles (right) on down to Stowe Hollow. While not as challenging as hiking the complete Skyline Trail, this option does offer an interesting hike.

Green Mountain Club

For the last hundred years, the Green Mountain Club has maintained the Long Trail, the footpath that stretches along Vermont's high peaks from Massachusetts to Canada. In 1910, Vermont Academy Headmaster James P. Taylor stood on the summit of Stratton Mountain and looked northward along the ridgeline of the Green Mountains. He envisioned a hiking trail through Vermont that would provide opportunities to take pleasure in the surrounding mountains. From this vision, the Green Mountain Club was born. Between 1910 and 1931, the club's first members built the Long Trail from Massachusetts to Quebec, establishing the nation's first long-distance hiking trail. Today, the Green Mountain Club remains a vibrant member-based, volunteer-powered nonprofit organization that works to con-

serve and maintain over 445 miles of Long Trail system and foster environmental stewardship through education. Based in Waterbury Center, the Green Mountain Club Visitor Center offers nature walks along the Short Trail, hiking guides, and expert advice. Resources are also available online at www.greenmountainclub.org.

Trail sign at GMC Headquarters

Heading south on the Long Trail, descending the Forehead
Photo by Alden Pellett

25 Worcester Mountain 3,293'

Worcester Mountain is probably the least-visited of the Worcester Range peaks, but it offers a good hike to an open summit. The blue-blazed trail crosses numerous small streams as it gradually increases in steepness. At about the halfway point, you walk between two boulders. The steeper upper portion of the trail ascends along exposed rock ledge to the top where there are views of the Stowe area and south along the spine of the Worcester Range. From the summit, the 9-mile **Skyline Trail** heads south along the ridgeline to Mt. Hunger.

3.5 hours and 5 miles round trip. Elevation gain: 1,970'
Approach: From the village of Worcester (on Route 12, north of Montpelier), drive up Minister Brook Road 1.5 miles to Hampshire Hill Road and turn right. At 3.9 miles, turn left and park at 4.1 miles.

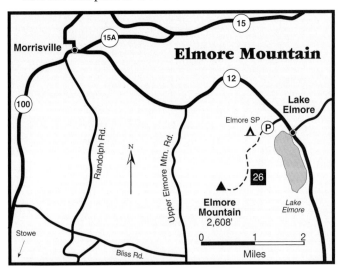

Lake Elmore from the fire tower on Elmore Mtn.   J. Hadden

26 Mount Elmore 2,608'

Although it is the lowest of the Worcester Range peaks described here, Mount Elmore is noticed immediately from most vantage points in the Stowe-Morrisville area because of its isolated setting at the end of the ridge. The peak is very prominent from Trapp Hill, for example. Climb the tower on the summit for great views of the lake, nearby farms, Mount Mansfield, and the mountains to the north such as Belvidere and Mount Pisgah. From the state park, follow the blue-blazed trail (it starts out as a service road) for about 2 miles to the open summit. Descend by the same route. Near the top, a half-mile spur trail leads right to **Balanced Rock**, a worthwhile addition to the basic hike.

2.5 hours and 4.2 miles round trip. Elev. gain: 1,450'
Approach: From Morrisville, drive east 4 miles on Route 12 to Lake Elmore State Park. Nominal fee charged.

3 Camel's Hump

One of Vermont's best known landmarks, Camel's Hump (4,083') offers possibly the finest mountain top in the state. Unspoiled by roads, ski areas, and communication antennas, its compact, rocky summit floats high above Burlington and the Champlain Valley. The Adirondacks are 40 miles to the west across Lake Champlain; the White Mountains of New Hampshire define the eastern horizon, and the Green Mountain chain stretches to the north and south.

27 From the west: the Burrows Trail

This popular route from Huntington represents the closest route for those coming from Burlington. From the parking lot, the well-maintained Burrows Trail immediately enters a hardwood forest, climbing moderately and steadily. The trail is more difficult higher up, with a prolonged steep and rocky section starting at about 1.5 miles. The slope slackens shortly before intersecting the Long Trail (2.1 miles) at a small clearing, 0.3 miles from the top. This is a good spot to eat, relax, and put on more clothes as it is likely to be cooler on the summit. From the clearing, turn right (south) on the **Long Trail** and scramble up the final very steep rocks, coming out into the open just below the summit. This last section is dramatic, as you suddenly emerge from dense woods to huge views of the Champlain Valley and the Adirondacks. Once on the summit the panoramic view—in fair weather—will test your mountain identifying skills for a good while. You might want to continue down below the summit to find secluded spots: This is a busy place on good weather days. Descend by the same route or do the loop variation, as described next.

Camel's Hump from Huntington   John Hadden

4 hours and 4.8 miles round trip. Elevation gain: 1,950'
Approach: From the traffic light in Richmond village, drive south 9 miles through Huntington to Huntington Center. Turn left on Camel's Hump Road and follow it 3.5 miles to the end.

Forest City Trail variation: Immediately after starting out on the Burrows Trail, turn right and descend on the 0.2-mile connector trail to the **Forest City Trail**. Here head left and climb up to **Wind Gap** on the LT at 1.4 miles. **Montclair Glen Lodge** is just to the right, and the top is north (left) along a demanding and very interesting 2-mile section of the LT. The final portion is spectacular, offering a fun scramble (traverse left) along the base of the summit cliff before the final climb on easy slabs to the summit. Descend by the Burrows Trail. This is a classic way to do Camel's Hump.
5 hours and 6 miles round trip. Elevation gain: 2,200'

28 From the east: the Monroe Trail

Probably the most popular route up Camel's Hump, the Monroe Trail (formerly Forestry Trail) is the natural route for those coming from the east. A wide, comfortable trail, especially in the first mile, it passes the **Dean Trail** at 1.3 miles and higher up, crosses the **Alpine Trail** at 2.5 miles. (The Alpine Trail traverses the east flank of the mountain, from the Long Trail north of the summit to a point on the LT at the base of the cliffs on the mountain's south side.) After 3.1 miles, the Monroe Trail ends on the Long Trail, at the clearing just north of the summit. The Burrows Trail, approaching from the west, ends here also. Now head south (left) on the **Long Trail** for 0.3 mile up steep and rocky terrain to the bare summit. For many, this is the best mountain top in the state. If it's breezy on top, you can usually find shelter behind a rock outcropping. Descend the same route: LT off the summit, then right on the Monroe Trail.

4 hours and 6.8 miles round trip. Elevation gain: 1,800'
Approach: From Waterbury (I-89, exit 10), take Rt. 2 east through Waterbury, turn right on Rt. 100, and then immediately right again onto River Rd. Follow it 4 miles, then turn left and continue (climbing) for 3.5 miles to the parking area.

Dean Trail variation: 1.3 miles up the Monroe Trail, the **Dean Trail** branches left to **Wind Gap** and the Long Trail. From Wind Gap, head right on the **Long Trail** for 1.7 miles to the top. The trail is quite steep and rough just above Wind Gap, followed by an easy section, before a prolonged steep climb up to the base of the final cliffs which are skirted to the left. (The scant remains of a B-24 bomber that crashed in 1944 can be seen a short way down the **Alpine Trail**.) The final climb up summit slabs makes for a great finish.

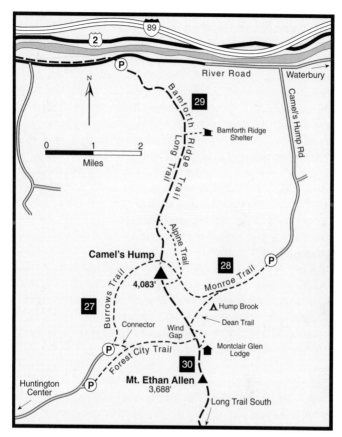

Descend north on the Long Trail, turning (right) down the **Monroe Trail**, 0.3 mile below the top. The loop offers more variety and more walking than the simple up-and-down.

About 5 hours, 7.5 miles. Elevation gain: 1,800'

Maps: Mad River Valley or Northern Vermont Hiking (Map Adventures); Vermont's Long Trail (GMC)

Camel's Hump 55

29 Bamforth Ridge Trail (Long Trail)

Although it receives a fraction of the traffic of the Burrows and Monroe Trails, the Bamforth Ridge Trail is in excellent condition. Starting at an elevation of only 350', it climbs steadily, at times quite steeply, to gain the top of the steep northern end of Bamforth Ridge. After about 1.5 hours, you reach the first of several open, ledgy sections with good views of the Hump and vistas to the east and west. From here, the trail takes on a more undulating character, crossing numerous open areas with good views. About 2.5 miles from the road, you will reach the spur trail (left, 0.2 mile) to the **Bamforth Ridge Shelter** (built in 2002) which has replaced Gorham Lodge. The final stiff climb of over 1,000' takes you past the **Alpine Trail** (on the left) and on to the summit 1.1 miles beyond the Alpine Trail intersection. Descend by the same route or by one of the other trails. This route has the most vertical gain of any hike in Vermont.

7-8 hours, 11.8 miles round trip. Elevation gain: 4,000'

Approach: Cross the Jonesville bridge (from US 2, east of Richmond) and drive east (left) on River Road for 3.5 miles to the small parking area on the right.

30 Mount Ethan Allen 3,680'

Ethan Allen is the peak just south of Camel's Hump. Ethan Allen does not rise above treeline, but it does offer some good views, especially north to Camel's Hump. From the Huntington side, hike up the Forest City Trail to the Long Trail (2.2 miles). **Montclair Glen Lodge** is a hundred yards or so south on the Long Trail. From here it is one mile and 1000' of climbing (at times steep) to the summit of Ethan Allen.

4 hours, 6.4 miles round trip. Gain: 1,600'

Approach: Same as for Burrows Trail, page 52.

On Bamforth Ridge, Camel's Hump in the distance J. Gange

Skier at Wind Gap, south of Camel's Hump   Jared Gange

Winter Activity on Camel's Hump

In winter, hikers and backcountry skiers are very active on this mountain. The Burrows, Monroe, Forest City, and Dean trails all seem to receive regular attention from skiers and snowshoers. It is frequently possible to hike quite pleasantly on a packed trail to the top of Camel's Hump in the middle of winter. The Burrows Trail has become popular with sledders.

Telemarkers enjoy the steep slopes on the east side of the mountain, especially off the Alpine Trail. The Monroe/Dean Trail route to the beaver pond below Wind Gap is a favorite among snowshoers.

Coming from the south, the **Catamount Ski Trail** traverses the west side of the mountain at a low elevation (1,500') before descending north-facing **Honey Hollow** to River Road in Jonesville.

Outdoor winter activity in northern New England, especially at higher elevations or in remote locations, requires a significantly greater level of preparation and conditioning than trips over the same terrain in the summer. There are various factors to consider: The days are much shorter (i.e. early darkness); there is a potential for rapid deterioration in conditions (drop in temperature, strong winds, reduced visibility, changing snow conditions); and it is generally more difficult to find and follow trails in winter. Perhaps the most surprising difference between summer and winter is the extreme variability of winter conditions. What was easy and fun last week, or just an hour ago, can turn into a very serious undertaking. Please see the chapter on backcountry skiing for more information on Catamount Trail sections and other backcountry ski tours.

4 The Mad River Valley

Home of the Sugarbush and Mad River Glen ski areas, the "Valley" offers good hiking, including two or three classic Vermont trips. In particular, the section of the Long Trail between Lincoln Gap and Appalachian Gap is something most hikers will want to do. This sharply-defined, at times quite narrow, 11-mile ridge includes Mount Abraham, Mount Lincoln, Mount Ellen, and the top of Mad River Glen, thus it crests all three ski areas. Waitsfield and Warren are the two towns in the Mad River Valley. Some of the hikes in this chapter start on the Lincoln (west) side of the range.

31 Mount Abraham 4,006'

The lowest of Vermont's five mountains over 4,000', Mount Abraham just barely pokes above the tree line. It is a great trip for kids who are up for 4 to 5 hours of hiking. For many kids, Mount Abe is the first "real" hike. From **Lincoln Gap**, follow the **Long Trail** north over varied terrain, passing **Battell Shelter** at 1.7 miles and reaching the summit at 2.6 miles. At the Battell Shelter, the Battell Trail joins from the left: It originates in Lincoln. The final section of the trail is steeper in spots and involves a little easy scrambling up rock slabs. Once on the top, the superb view is known for giving a sensation of peering straight down on the farms of Lincoln. Needless to say, this is a fantastic spot during fall foliage.

4 hours and 5.2 miles round trip. Elevation gain: 1,700'
Approach: From Warren, drive up Lincoln Gap Road, and park in one of several parking lots just below the height of land in Lincoln Gap. From the west, drive to Lincoln and follow the Lincoln Gap highway to the Gap.

After-hike reward at Bristol Falls
Jared Gange

32 Sunset Ledge

This short, out-and-back hike south on the Long Trail from **Lincoln Gap** requires about 40 minutes of walking each way. The ledges are just off the trail to the right. This is a dramatic spot with great views of Lincoln, and in the distance, the Adirondacks. The hike has some steep sections in the beginning but is easier higher up.

1.5 hours and 2 miles round trip

Approach: Drive to Lincoln Gap from Warren or Lincoln. The Lincoln Gap Road is very steep and winding and is closed for the season as soon as snow falls.

33 Mount Abraham via the Battell Trail

The route up Mount Abraham from the Lincoln side is somewhat longer and involves more climbing than from Lincoln Gap, elevation 2,410'. The trail climbs surprisingly moderately over its 2-mile length and ends on the Long Trail, just south of **Battell Shelter**. From here, continue north on the Long Trail to the summit. The trail breaks into the open just below the top. Return by the same trail. The arctic grasses and other vegetation that grow at the summit area are easily damaged by foot traffic and regenerate very slowly. Therefore, hikers are asked to keep off the grass!

5 hours and 5.8 miles round trip. Elevation gain: 2,550'
Approach: From Lincoln, drive north on Quaker St. for 0.5 mile, turning right on Elder Rd. Follow signs to trailhead.

Mount Abe as seen from Lincoln   Jared Gange

34 Jerusalem Trail up Mt. Ellen (4,083')

This is a fine west-side approach, similar to the Battell Trail on Mt. Abraham. From the car, follow the trail for 2.5 miles to the ridge and the Long Trail. The trail is gentle in its lower section, then steepens as it nears the Long Trail. From here it is 1.8 miles (right) to the top of Mt. Ellen, and the 0.2-mile spur trail to **Glen Ellen Lodge** is just to the north. It is 1.7 miles north to the top of the single chairlift at Mad River Glen (good views).

5-6 hours, 8.6 miles round trip. Elevation gain: 2,580'
Approach: From Rt. 116, drive 3.3 miles up Route 17 and bear right on Jerusalem Rd., then left on Jim Dwire Rd. at 4.6 miles. The trailhead is on the right after 0.5 mile.

Dead fir trees near tree line   David Seaver

35 Lincoln Gap to Appalachian Gap

Between these two gaps, or mountain passes, the crest of the Green Mountains forms a sharp ridgeline that keeps a high elevation. The Long Trail runs along the ridgecrest: this section of the LT is a classic. Although the ridge is generally densely wooded, the trail itself is challenging, and there are enough viewpoints to make this a very worthwhile excursion. It can be done in a single day by fit hikers. Others may want to spread the trip over two days. From Lincoln Gap, at 2,410 feet, take the **Long Trail** north past the **Battell Shelter** (room for 8) to the summit of **Mount Abraham** (4,006'). A comfortable time for this first portion is 2 hours. From here, it is 2 miles to the top of **Sugarbush Ski Area** (Castlerock Lift). Continuing along the narrow, forested ridge, cross the top of **Mount Ellen** (4,083') and the **Sugarbush North Ski Area** (excellent views) after about 4 hours of walking and 6.5 miles. (If it is necessary to cut the trip short, descend to the base of the ski area.) After descending from Mount Ellen, pass the Jerusalem Trail on the left, and at 8 miles, the short spur trail (right 0.3 mile) to **Glen Ellen Lodge** (sleeps 8). A mile farther on, you reach the top of **Mad River Glen Ski Area** and **Stark's Nest**, a rustic building from which there are good views. From here it is 2.5 miles over relatively easy terrain to Route 17 in Appalachian Gap.

7-8 hours, 11.6 miles. Elevation gain northbound: 2,520'
Approach: Start from Lincoln Gap or Appalachian Gap. Appalachian Gap is on Route 17, 6 miles west of Waitsfield. Route 17 is kept open year round, but Lincoln Gap is not.

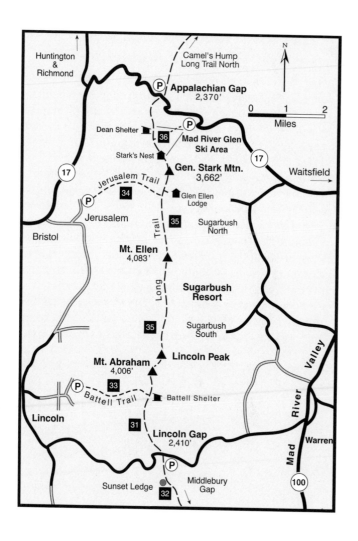

36 Mad River Glen Ski Area and General Stark Mountain (3,662')

The goal here is to climb up the ski runs to the top of Mad River Glen's legendary single chairlift. This is the lift on your left, as seen from the base of the ski area. There are only a few lifts here, so it is possible to hike out of sight of cables and lift towers. There are beautiful large maples and birches, and the woods are well-groomed, creating the effect of a steep park. At the top of the lift (3,644'), there is an old, but refurbished building (**Stark's Nest**), with a deck that is a good place to relax and enjoy the view. Mad River's runs are very steep, and there are occasional cliffs, thus it is a good idea to take it easy when descending. Take the ski run just south of the top when starting down. **General Stark** Mountain is a short (0.6 mile, 20 minutes) walk south on the Long Trail and is slightly higher than Stark's Nest.

3-4 hours, 3-4 miles round trip. Elevation gain: 2,000'

Approach: From Waitsfield, drive west on Route 17 to the large parking area at the base of Mad River Glen Ski Area.

Yellow spotted salamander John Gange

Leaping down Burnt Rock   Jared Gange

37 Burnt Rock Mountain 3,160'

This rolling trail climbs through creeks and hardwood forest, connecting with an old road and then following it up the valley. Big rock outcroppings are abundant as the trail climbs, turns south, and then levels out to reveal good views of Burnt Rock summit (on the right). The **Hedgehog Brook Trail** then steepens for a short time before connecting with the **Long Trail**, which winds through softwoods. The trail heads steeply up here; the rocks and hemlocks make this section interesting. The trail then opens up with various views on the way to the summit with its full panorama.

3.5 hours, 5.2 miles. Elevation gain: 2,090'

Approach: From Waitsfield drive north on VT 100 for 3.4 miles then turn left on to North Fayston Road. Continue straight at Big Basin Road (7.5 miles). Reach parking area at 8.4 miles. The trail begins on the left.

Is the Water Safe To Drink?

When you are hot and thirsty, it's hard to resist a sparkling brook. Used to be you could drink water safely from streams and rivulets. But today, with the **Giardia lambia parasite**—a widespread microscopic organism—the recommendation is to treat all drinking water. One option is to boil it for about five minutes. Another is filtering; be sure to have the correct kind of filter. Iodine and chlorine treatments do not destroy the parasite.

The symptoms are nasty: diarrhea, gas, stomach cramps, weight loss, and nausea. They can be with you for months even years, so this isn't something to take lightly! Animals and people pass the parasite through feces, thus hikers should bury waste at least 200' from any water source.

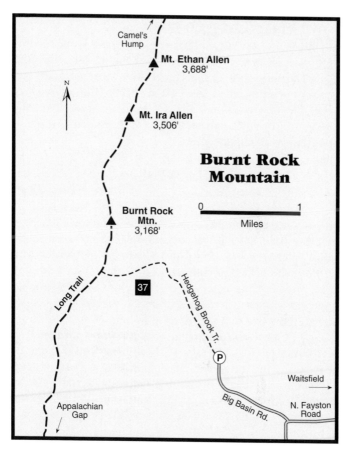

Maps: *Mad River Valley or Northern Vermont Hiking (Map Adventures) and Vermont's Long Trail (GMC); Addison County (Huntington Graphics)*

5 Burlington

Vermont's largest urban area happens to be located near some of the state's best hiking: Mt. Mansfield, Camel's Hump, and Mount Hunger. But there are good hiking and walking areas within the greater Burlington area itself. Shelburne's Mount Philo is a classic short hike, and the gentle, open terrain of Shelburne Farms offers some of the finest walking anywhere.

38 Eagle Mountain 574'

Spectacular views ·of Lake Champlain reward the hiker for trekking up the gentle backside of this lakeside bluff. Milton's **Eagle Mountain Natural Area** has a well-marked trail network, and the easy terrain makes the hikes accessible to all ages. A combination of trails #1 and #2 gets you to both the (wooded) summit and clifftop Hoyt Overlook with views of the lake and South Hero. Cedar Island and Fishbladder Island lie below, while the rugged Adirondacks define the western horizon.

Loop: 1 hour and 1.8 miles. Total elevation gain: 400'

Approach: From I-89 exit 17, head west on US 2 for 2.4 miles to Bear Trap Rd. Drive north, at 1.8 miles keep straight, then immediately left on a gravel road. Follow this 2.6 mi. (cross Everest Rd. after 2 mi.) to Cold Spring Rd. and turn left. The trailhead is on the right in 0.2 mi.

39 Mount Philo 980'

A popular short hike with sweeping views of the Champlain Valley, Mount Philo is a moderate little jaunt, although steep. All visitors are charged a nominal usage fee during the summer season. Hikers can choose between the paved road or a steep and rough trail. From the gate, the trail heads (left)

View from Mt. Philo over Lake Champlain   Jared Gange

through woods, traversing the west side of the mountain. It ascends steeply, crosses the road then gets steeper with short switchbacks. At a fork (sign) you have the option to head right and traverse along the base of cliffs. Staying on the main trail it's not far to the top. The trail comes out at the western overlook. From there it's a short distance to the main overlook. Both have excellent views. The summit area has picnic tables and camping sites. Follow the road or the trail back down to the parking area. Probably because of the steep and rough nature of the trail, the paved road is the preferred route for most walkers.

1-2 hours and 2.3 miles. Total elevation gain: 350'

Approach: From Burlington take Route 7 south through Shelburne and Charlotte. Approximately 2.5 miles past Ferry Rd. in Charlotte, turn east (left) onto State Park Road. Drive 0.6 mile to the park entrance and parking lot.

Map: *Burlington Hike & Bike Map (Map Adventures)*

40 Lone Tree Hill, Shelburne Farms

Originally a vast farm estate, Shelburne Farms and some of its important buildings (including some incredible barns) are now open to the public. Shelburne Farms has a well-signed trail network. A trail map is included in the nominal entrance fee. This short, introductory walk offers sweeping views with relatively little exertion. The **Farm Trail** begins to the right of the Welcome Center and is marked with blue reflectors on stakes. An easy 15-minute walk brings you to the gigantic **Farm Barn** (shown above), an architectural treasure. The trail passes to the right of the barn and continues 0.3 mile to the top of Lone Tree Hill. From this grassy knoll, the Adirondacks, Lake Champlain and much of Shelburne Farms are yours! It's a great spot for a picnic. Return by the same route or use the map to put together a longer variation. The Farm Trail Loop is 4.25 miles.

1 hour and 2 miles. Total elevation gain: 150'

Approach: From Shelburne village on Route 7, head west on Harbor Road 1.5 miles to the Shelburne Farms entrance and Welcome Center. Park here, on the right.

Photo at left: Farm Barn, on the trail to Lone Tree Hill J. Gange

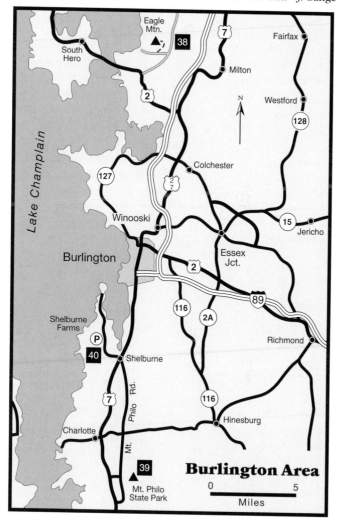

6 Middlebury and Brandon

The hikes for this area are spread around: Snake Mountain rises out of the farming country west of Middlebury; Rattlesnake Point is high above Lake Dunmore; Mount Horrid Overlook is in Brandon Gap; and the Robert Frost Lookout is reached by hiking along the top of Middlebury College's Snow Bowl Ski Area. The TAM, The Trail Around Middlebury, shown on the map below, is a 16-mile footpath that encircles the village of Middlebury. Last, we give various hikes that use the Long Trail between Middlebury Gap and South Lincoln.

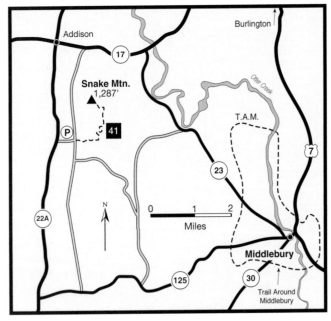

Adirondack view from Addison (near Snake Mtn.)   J. Gange

41 Snake Mountain 1,287'

Snake Mountain is a distinctive north-south running ridge of hills that rises almost 1,000' above the farms of Addison County. The views of Lake Champlain and the Adirondacks from the top of the cliffs are beautiful, especially in the late afternoon. From the gate, walk up the pleasant woods road. After a "T" (head left), the route steepens and zig-zags up the mountainside. Once you are on the ridge, watch for the side trail (left) out onto the top of the cliffs, where there is an old foundation. You might see ravens gliding above the line of cliffs. Return by the same route.

2.5 hours and 3.6 miles round trip. Elevation gain: 950'
Approach: From Middlebury, take Route 125 to Route 22A then drive north 4.5 miles to Wilmarth Road. Turn right and continue to the T-intersection with Mountain Road. The trail up Snake begins on the gated woods road right at the intersection, and the trailhead parking is 50 yards left on Mountain Road.

42 Abbey Pond 1,700'

With its marshlands, hemlocks, and birch, Abbey Pond is a lovely spot to have a picnic and relax. You'll find small islands and brush along the edges of the water, giving the pond a cozy feel. The Robert Frost Mountain overlooks the pond and wetlands, which provide habitat for all kinds of wildlife. From the parking area follow the well-marked, blue-blazed trail, which follows an old road. This moderate trail with one steep section crosses a stream bed a few times; you will see cascades as well.

2 hours and 3.8 miles. Elevation gain 520'

Approach: From Bristol, drive south on Rt. 116 for 8.4 miles. A sign on the left (east) directs you to the parking area down a dirt road. Park at the old sugar house.

43 Bristol Cliffs Wilderness

This is a wilderness area southeast of Bristol. There are 3,740 acres of forest with cliffs overlooking the Champlain Valley and a couple of ponds and multiple little streams. The Wilderness is a fun place to spend time in the woods away from people. Because this is a wilderness area, visitors must be sure to preserve the natural character of the area and to protect the plant and animal species in their undisturbed habitat. For more information on the Wilderness, the Forest Service has free pamphlets.

Time and distance: variable Elevation gain: 800 - 1000'

Approach: From West Lincoln, a wilderness sign directs you south onto York Hill Road. Drive 1.7 miles to a 10-car parking area on the right. The small footpath soon disappears in the woods.

Maps: Vermont's Long Trail (GMC); Addison County (Huntington Graphics)

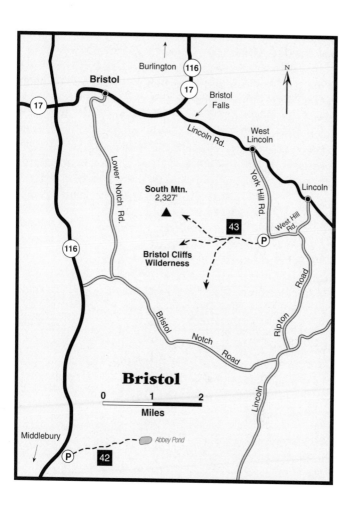

44 Emily Proctor-Cooley Glen Loop

A solid day's hike, this loop is formed by two access trails to the Long Trail and the connecting 5.6-mile section along the trail itself. Although the route is almost entirely wooded, there is a fine, open ledge near the top of Mount Roosevelt called **Killington Overlook**. From the trailhead, take the trail to **Cooley Glen Shelter**, reaching the **Long Trail** after 3.4 miles. Turn right, heading south along the LT, passing Killington Overlook at 7 miles and reaching **Emily Proctor Shelter** at 9 miles. From here, it is 3.5 miles down the Emily Proctor Trail to your starting point. The mountains traversed on this section of the Long Trail are: Mt. Cleveland, Mt. Roosevelt, and Mt. Wilson (at 3,745', the highest).

7-8 hours, 12.5 mile loop. Elevation gain: 3,120'

Approach: From Lincoln (east of Bristol), drive through South Lincoln to Forest Road #201 (USFS signs). Turn left and proceed to the trailhead and parking.

To climb **Breadloaf Mountain** (3,835'), hike to Emily Proctor Shelter, then south on the LT for 0.7 mile. A short spur trail to the west leads to good views from this summit, the highest between Lincoln and Middlebury Gaps. (For a shorter route to Breadloaf (7 miles round trip), see the trail description to **Skylight Pond**.)

45 Skylight Pond

The **Skylight Pond Trail** provides quick access to **Skyline Lodge**, a nice cabin nestled above Skylight Pond. Both are just east of the Long Trail. From the parking area, walk up the gentle woods road for about 20 minutes, when it will begin to steepen. After a steady climb, there are views through the trees just before reaching the Long Trail (2.3 miles). Straight on is the trail to the cabin and the pond. To

Falls of Lana   David Seaver

your right (on the LT south), the spur trail (right) to Battell
Lookout, with good views west, is 250' away. Descend by
the same route.

4 hours, 5 miles, elevation gain: 1,400' (Skyline Lodge)
Approach: From Ripton (east of Middlebury on Rt. 125),
take Forest Rd. #59 (left) 3.6 miles to the trailhead.

46 Robert Frost Lookout

From Middlebury Gap, hike south on the **Long Trail**, passing through the Middlebury College Snow Bowl Ski Area. Ski trails are crossed seven times. Actually, the best views on the entire trip are from the first and last of these ski trail crossings. The first clearing has excellent views to the west, and the last one has good views to the east. After leaving the ski area, the trail steepens, soon reaching Robert Frost Lookout with a view to the west. After passing a few more minor lookouts, you reach the viewless, wooded summit of **Worth Mountain**, 3,234'.

4.5 hours and 5.4 miles round trip. Gain: 1,300'

Approach: From Middlebury, drive to East Middlebury then up Route 125 to Middlebury Gap.

47 Cape Lookout Mountain 3,298'

This hike includes the spectacular views of **Brandon Gap** from popular **Mount Horrid Overlook**. From the parking area, cross the highway, and following the Long Trail north up through a fine birch forest, reach the spur trail (right) to the overlook after about 20 minutes. Walk out on the ledge for the view. *Note:* Because of Peregrine Falcon nesting, access to the top of the cliff might be closed from spring to late summer. Continue on the LT over **Mount Horrid** to the top of Cape Lookout Mountain. There are a couple of interesting viewpoints along the way. Return by the same route.

3 hours, 3.4 miles round trip. Elev. gain: 1,300'

Approach: From Brandon, drive east 8 miles on Rt. 73 to Brandon Gap. Parking is on the south side of Rt. 73. From Rochester (on Rt. 100), Brandon Gap is 10 miles west.

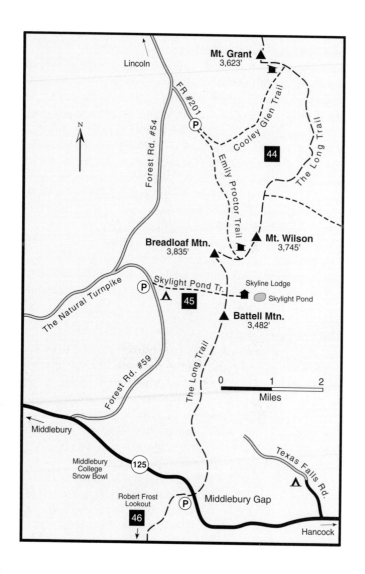

48 Rattlesnake Point

This moderate hike leads to spectacular views of Lake Dunmore and Silver Lake. Not an actual summit, Rattlesnake Point is a series of ledges perched high above the lake. From the popular **Falls of Lana** (only about 15-20 minutes walk), follow signs to Rattlesnake Cliff — it is about 1.6 miles farther on. The excellent trail climbs briskly then eases before climbing very steeply for a short distance to the spur trail, which leads left to the ledge overlooks. Both viewpoints should be visited, although the south lookout has a wider and more varied view. Unlike many precipitous dropoffs, these roomy ledges are inviting places to relax.

3 hours and 4.5 miles round trip. Elevation gain: 1,100'

Approach: A short distance south of the park entrance are two parking areas on the left. Both are trailheads for the Falls of Lana, but the second (farther) one is the main one.

49 Falls of Lana

A nice swimming destination, the soothing sounds of water reward you as you approach the falls with its large pool and dramatic cliffs. From the parking loop (on the right) follow an access road along easy grades up to the falls and Silver Lake. You will pass stones and boulders along the route, reaching a clearing with views of Lake Dunmore just before you reach the falls.

15-20 minutes, 1 mile round trip.

Approach: Drive 6 miles north of VT 73 in Forestdale or 3.5 miles east of US 7. Signs mark the parking area on the east side of the road, 0.2 mile south of the Branbury State Park Entrance, on the east side of Lake Dunmore. A short distance south of the entrance are two parking areas on the left. Both are starting points for Falls of Lana.

Lake Dunmore and Branbury State Park

Nestled at the foot of the Green Mountains, between Middlebury and Brandon, Lake Dunmore is a very popular swimming and boating spot. Of the several hikes in the area, Rattlesnake Point offers the best views. The less strenuous hike to peaceful Silver Lake is also a favorite.

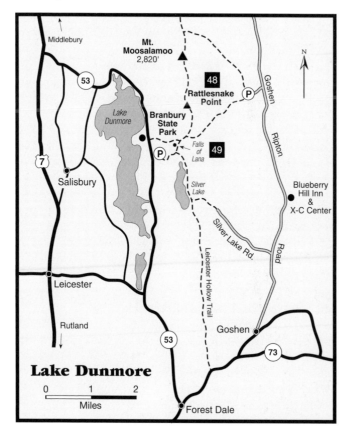

7 Killington and Rutland

Killington Peak, together with its various satellite peaks, is one of Vermont's largest mountains. It is also the home of the East's largest ski area, and the ski trails offer the hiker open slopes with great views. The **Long Trail/Appalachian Trail** passes through here, and just north of busy Route 4, the trails separate — the AT heads east to New Hampshire, and the LT continues north to Canada.

50 Killington Peak 4,241'

The most popular hiking trail up Vermont's second highest mountain is the **Bucklin Trail** (blue blazes), which ascends from the west. The first 2 miles are along a gentle woods road and make for easy walking. After branching (right) off the road, the trail climbs very steeply all the way to **Cooper Lodge** on the **Long Trail**, slackening only a short ways below the lodge. From here, continue for 0.2 mile (steep) to the open, rocky summit with fine views in all directions, although various antennas clutter the view to the southeast. Descend by the same trail.

5-6 hours, 7.2 miles round trip. Elevation gain: 2,480'
Approach: 5 miles east on Route 4 (from Rt. 7 in Rutland), turn right on Wheelerville Road. Park after 4 miles.

51 Killington via ski trails

From the Killington Base Lodge, hike up under the K1 Express Gondola. As you ascend the very steep, grassy ski run, a fine view gradually unfolds. This "alpine" hiking terrain offers a pleasant change from our typical forest trails.

Time and approach: Drive to the upper end of the Killington Access Road. The hike up will take 1-2 hours. The chairlift is in operation throughout the summer.

Pico Peak from Killington's summit   Lisa Densmore

52 Pico Peak 3,957'

Although lower than Killington, Pico's location and attractive symmetrical shape make it more noticeable, especially from the Rutland side. The peak offers good hiking with great views from the summit. Pico is climbed easily by hiking the ski trails. For the **Sherburne Pass Trail** route, head south from the trailhead at Sherburne Pass. After about 20 minutes, there is a short side trail to the top of a chairlift and a view. At 2.5 miles you reach **Pico Camp**, a small cabin for Long Trail hikers. From here, the **Pico Link** side trail branches right and climbs steeply for 0.4 mile to the top.

4 hours, 5.8 miles round trip. Elevation gain: 1,810'

Approach: Park on Sherburne Pass across from the Long Trail Inn.

53 Deer Leap Rock

The interesting cliffs directly above Sherburne Pass on Route 4 provide a dramatic view of **Pico Peak** and the highway just below. To get to the cliff top overlook, follow the blue-blazed **Sherburne Pass Trail** north from the right side of the **Long Trail Inn**. Until recently the Sherburne Pass Trail was the Long Trail/Appalachian Trail. Now, after re-routing of the LT/AT, it simply links Route 4 to the **Appalachian Trail**, after the AT has separated from the LT. In any event, after a steep and rocky start, the Sherburne Pass Trail brings you to the AT after 0.5 mile of walking. Head left on the AT 200' to pick up the **Deer Leap Overlook Trail**. Follow this 0.4 mile to the spur trail (left, 0.2 mile) that leads to the famed overlook. Return by the same route.

1-2 hours and 2.2 miles round trip. Elevation gain: 650'
Approach: Park next to the Long Trail Inn at Sherburne Pass on Route 4, about 9 miles east of Rutland.

54 Shrewsbury Peak 3,720'

This eastern satellite peak of Killington offers good hiking in a less-visited area. From the parking area, the blue-blazed **Shrewsbury Peak Trail** makes a short climb then descends briefly before resuming its steady climb to the top. There are no viewpoints along the way but once at the summit you will enjoy excellent views to the south. Descend by the same trail. For a longer variation: From the top of Shrewsbury, it is just a short way to the **Black Swamp Trail**, and about 2 miles on to the Long Trail. The Black Swamp Trail descends (right) for 1.5 miles to Black Swamp Road. It is then about 2.2 miles by road back to the base of the Shrewsbury Peak Trail.

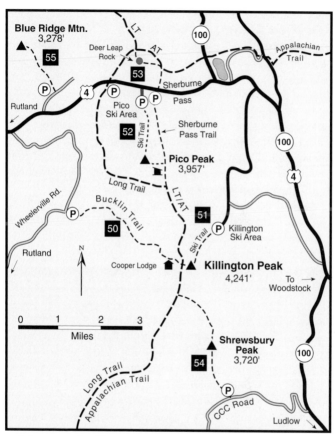

Blue Ridge Mtn.
3,278'
55

LT

AT

100

Appalachian Trail

Deer Leap Rock

53

Sherburne Pass

4

P

P

P P

Rutland

Pico Ski Area

52

Ski Trail

Sherburne Pass Trail

100

4

Pico Peak
3,957'

Long Trail

LT/AT

Wheelerville Rd.

Bucklin Trail

P

50

51

P Killington Ski Area

Rutland

Ski Trail

N

Cooper Lodge

Killington Peak
4,241'

To → Woodstock

0   1   2   3
Miles

Shrewsbury Peak
3,720'

100

54

Long Trail

Appalachian Trail

P

CCC Road

Ludlow →

3 hours, 3.6 miles round trip. Elevation gain: 1,500'
Approach: From Rt. 100, 3 miles south of Rt. 4, turn right on the CCC Road for 3.3 miles to parking on the right. From the west, the trailhead is 3 miles east of North Shrewsbury.

Map: *Vermont's Long Trail (GMC); Killington Peak Map (GMC); Killington Area Hiking Trail Map (GMC)*

55 Blue Ridge Mountain 3,278'

Located northwest of Killington and Pico, the rocky summit of Blue Ridge Mountain offers views of Rutland, Killington, and nearby mountains. From Turnpike Road, follow blue blazes along a woods road past a large camp building and onto the **Canty Trail**. The trail is gradual at first, then climbs steeply along a brook for a while before climbing over easier terrain through some nice woods to a clearing and the summit. Continue a short way beyond the summit to be rewarded with better views. Descend by the same trail.

3.5 hours and 4.8 miles round trip. Gain: 1,500'

Approach: About 6 miles east of Rutland, turn left off Route 4 on to Turnpike Road and proceed for 0.7 mile to a gated road on the left. Park on the road shoulder.

Green Mountain National Forest

Vermont's Green Mountain National Forest, our only national forest, comprises 350,000 acres. The northern section runs along the Green Mountains from US Route 4 north to Bristol, while the southern section runs south from Wallingford to the Bennington area. The Forest Supervisor's office is located on Route 7 in Rutland, and district offices are found in Middlebury, Rochester, and Manchester. Each office maintains a Visitor Information Center, which offers free handouts on outdoor activities: hiking, biking, fishing, camping, canoeing, wildlife viewing, cross country skiing, and snowmobiling. Rangers are on hand to answer questions. In Vermont, the Forest Service maintains access roads (Forest Service Roads), campgrounds, and over 500 miles of trails; thus it is an important part of the outdoor recreation picture in Vermont.

The Long Trail Inn and Deer Leap Rock   Jared Gange

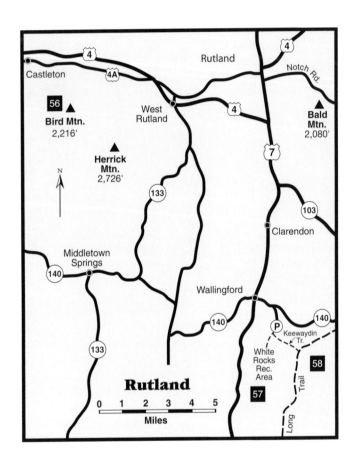

Rutland

0 1 2 3 4 5
Miles

Bird Mountain from the south   Jared Gange

56 Bird Mountain 2,216'

Bird Mountain is an impressive, very steep, small mountain just south of Route 4, between Castleton and Rutland. Its high south face is almost vertical and is both a peregrine falcon nesting area and a launch area for hang gliders. The north side was home to a ski area in the 1960s. There are various routes to the top, but none are well-documented. By following Birdseye Road to the picnic area mentioned below, it is then possible to follow a series of rough trails to the top. The mountain can also be climbed from the east from another road named Birdseye, and also via ATV trails.

2-3 hours, roundtrip distance 3 miles, gain 1,050'
Approach: From US Route 4 (west of Rutland) take exit 5 and head east on Route 4A (back toward Rutland) for 2.4 miles to Birdseye Road. Follow this gravel road south for 3 miles along the west side of the mountain to an open area with a picnic shelter and old cemetery.

57 White Rocks (Ice Bed Trail)

This destination—an area of jumbled boulders where lingering ice creates cool breezes—gives this hike its name. From the southwest corner of the picnic area, follow the blue-blazed trail. After crossing a brook, the path climbs a knoll (0.2 mile). On the left, a spur trail offers a nice view of White Rocks Cliffs, formed by glacial action. After a more expansive view of the cliff area greets you at 0.3 mile, the trail descends and joins a jeep trail. Go left to cross the stream. The Ice Beds, the source of the stream, are 0.5 mile farther.

1.5 hours. 0.3 mile to vista, 0.8 mile to Ice Beds.
Gain: 170' to vista, from the vistas to Ice Beds, -270'
Approach: From Wallingford, head east on VT Route 140. At 2.1 miles bear right and follow signs to White Rocks National Recreation Area.

58 White Rocks Cliffs (Keewaydin Trail)

The trail starts from the back of the parking lot and follows blue blazes up alongside Bully Brook. The Brook has two cascades about 0.5 mile into the trail. There are nice views to the north as the route ascends to the Long Trail. At the junction with the Long Trail, head south (right) for about 0.3 mile. Rock cairns and a sign mark the trail that descends 0.2 mile to the cliffs, with their splendid views to the south, west, north, and overlooking the ice beds. Here you will find interesting rock formations and multiple spots to sit and enjoy lunch. This trail may be closed at times because of Peregrine Falcon nesting.

Total time 2 hours, 2.6 miles, Elevation gain: 1,150'
Approach: From Wallingford at the junction with VT 140, head east on VT 140 2.1 miles. Bear right onto Sugar Road. Signs will direct you to the Forest Service picnic area.

Young hiker exploring the Ice Beds   Lisa Densmore

Mt. Zion from Hubbardton Battlefield   Jared Gange

Taconic Mountains Ramble

This is not a high elevation area, but it feels like one. It is hugely hilly with vast meadows that open up a shocking amount of sky and distant views. The Taconic Mountains Ramble is an extensive trail network near Rutland, just south of the Hubbardton Battlefield. The trails spread across the 420-acre property of the Davidsons, who always welcome visitors. The Ramble also features numerous waterfalls, panoramic views, rocky summits, open fields and a large Japanese Garden. A free trail map is available near the parking area. There is only one requirement: that visitors neither smoke nor build fires.

Mt. Zion Major 1,220'

A loop trail, slightly less than a mile, runs over the property's high point. From the parking area, walk toward the right-hand end of the house, and just before reaching the tool shed, bear right on the red-marked **Springs Trail**, which soon enters the woods. After 0.1 mile, pass the yellow-marked **Cave Trail**, and after a slight climb and a couple of switchbacks, pass (on your right) the **Cliff Trail**. (Featuring occasional steep ups-and-downs, it provides a challenging alternate route to the top of **Mt. Zion**, but can be dangerous for inexperienced hikers or children.) Staying on the Springs Trail, you reach the summit at 0.5 mile from your starting point. There are great views here: the Taconic Range to the east, the Battlefield to the north, and the Adirondacks of New York to the far northwest. From the summit continue down the **Mickie Trail**. It negotiates several switchbacks on narrow but secure ledges before descending through an interesting boulder field and then in a mellower fashion through woods back to the parking area. Total time for this hike is about 30 minutes of walking.

As a unique bonus, you should visit the **Japanese Garden**. It's a 90-second walk from the house, down the meadow to an arched bridge. With three ponds and five waterfalls, it is like no other garden in Vermont. There are also a number of other trails, plus two waterfall streams across the road.

Approach: From exit 5 on Route 4, west of Rutland, drive north on East Hubbardton Rd. (changes to Monument Hill Rd., no sign) for approx 6 miles to St. John Rd. (sign). Turn left and after 0.3 mile, left again onto a private drive. Continue for 0.6 mile to the parking area (sign).

8 Mount Ascutney Area

The isolated shape of Mount Ascutney (3,150') is one of Vermont's best-known landmarks. Located in the town of Windsor, near the Connecticut River, Ascutney is unchallenged by other peaks and is clearly visible for many miles throughout New Hampshire and Vermont. Although Ascutney is lower than many Vermont summits, its relative isolation and solid vertical rise contribute to make this one of the best mountain views in Vermont. In geologic terms, Mount Ascutney is a classic monadnock. Formerly the site of extensive granite quarrying and logging, Ascutney is today a recreation destination. In addition to Mount Ascutney Ski Area and Mount Ascutney State Park, there are four hiking trails to the top, a hang glider launch area and a paved toll road to the 2,750' level.

59 Ascutney via Weathersfield Trail

The blue-blazed Weathersfield Trail passes two cascades and numerous viewpoints on its varied route to the top. In particular, 84-foot-high **Crystal Cascade** (at 1.2 miles) is noteworthy, as it gives a glimpse of Ascutney's geologic origins. **Gus's Lookout** (2,700'), at 2.3 miles, is open to the south, and at 2.6 miles, a short spur trail leads to **West Peak** with its excellent views. Take the left fork just before the summit to reach the observation platform and its 360-degree vista. Descend by the same route. Mount Ascutney's mid-state location provides a perfect spot to view Vermont's Green Mountains, as well as the mountains of New Hampshire.

4 hours and 5.8 miles round trip. Elevation gain: 2,060'
Approach: Drive 3.3 miles west on Route 131 from the Ascutney exit on I-91, turn right on to Cascade Falls Rd., and follow signs to the trailhead parking.

View from Brownsville Rock on Mt. Ascutney   Lisa Densmore

60 Mount Ascutney via Brownsville Trail

An excellent and varied hike, the Brownsville Trail starts out steeply, then follows a moderately graded road to an old granite quarry. After negotiating some rougher terrain, the trail settles into a steady climb passing various viewpoints and joins with the **Windsor Trail** before reaching the summit observation tower. From a clearing 0.2 mile before the tower, a short spur leads right to **Brownsville Rock** with its bird's-eye view of the surrounding area. Descend by the same route or by the Windsor Trail (1.2-mile road section west along Rt. 44).

4.5 hours and 6.4 miles round trip. Gain: 2,400'

Approach: From the village of Windsor, drive 4.6 miles west on Route 44 and park in the small trailhead parking lot on the south side of the highway.

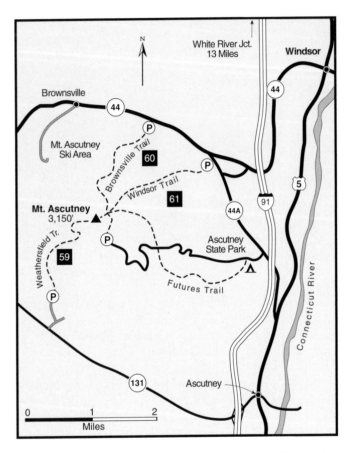

Maps: *Mt. Acutney State Park Recreation Guide; Killington Area Hiking Trail Map (GMC)*

61 Mount Ascutney via Windsor Trail

This popular trail is the most direct route to the top. From Route 44A, you start out in a field but soon enter the woods and climb more steeply. On this long-used route (white blazes), you pass the sites of old cabins and various dramatic episodes of yesteryear. At about 2.5 miles, the stone hut clearing is reached (take the short detour right to spectacular **Brownsville Rock**), and the summit platform, a 24-foot high truncated tower, is just beyond. Descend by the same trail or by Brownsville Trail. The distance between the two trailheads is 1.2 miles.

4.5 hours and 5.4 miles round trip. Gain: 2,520'

Approach: From Windsor, drive about 3.5 miles west on Route 44 to Route 44A. Then turn left on to Route 44A for a short distance to the trail parking lot on your right.

62 Okemo Mountain 3,343' (Ludlow)

From the tower on Okemo's summit, the hiker is rewarded by a 360-degree view of mountains near and far. Completed in 1993 by Vermont's Youth Conservation Corps, the **Healdville Trail** ascends the north side of the mountain over mixed terrain. The first third climbs moderately, followed by an easier section before the final steeper climb. Stay right at the junction near the top. Descend by the same trail.

4 hours and 5.8 miles round trip. Elevation gain: 1,940'

Approach: From Ludlow, drive north on Route 100 to Route 103. Continue 3 miles on Rt. 103 to Station Road, turn left, and proceed 0.8 mile to the trailhead parking.

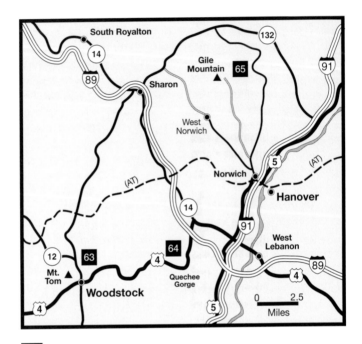

63 Mount Tom 1,250' (Woodstock)

A pleasant, very gently graded path, complete with occasional benches, leads to the top of Woodstock's local mountain. It is the sort of path you would expect to find on a mountainside in Europe. Pick up the trail at the rear of **Faulkner Park**, and after many switchbacks crest a knoll just below the summit. Continue a short ways on a steeper and rougher path to the actual top of Mt. Tom, where there are excellent views of Woodstock and the surrounding area.

2 hours and 3 miles round trip. Elevation gain: 550'
Approach: Drive or walk to Faulkner Park, on Mountain Avenue, across the covered bridge in Woodstock.

64 Quechee Gorge

Quechee Gorge is a 165-foot deep gorge of the Ottauquechee River. The vantage point from the Route 4 bridge provides an impressive view of what locals affectionately refer to as Vermont's "Little Grand Canyon". Hiking down into the gorge provides interesting perspectives. The **Quechee Gorge Trail** begins to the west of the parking area and, after bearing left, runs down to the water. Swim at your own risk, where the river's grade slackens, after the channel divides.

1 hour and 1 mile round trip. Elevation gain: 200'
Approach: From I-89, exit 2, follow US Route 4 west towards Woodstock. The gorge is 6 miles east of Woodstock and 5 miles west of I-89. When approaching from the east, park on the right side of the road, at the gift shops just before the bridge.

65 Gile Mountain 1,873'

This hike is a local favorite for residents of the Hanover-Norwich region. The blue-blazed trail leads over relatively easy terrain to a firetower. The firetower gets you above the trees and provides a panoramic view of the surrounding area: the Connecticut River Valley, the White Mountains, the Green Mountains, including nearby Mt. Ascutney. From the parking lot, the trail climbs through woods over easy terrain, crossing a powerline clearing at 0.3 miles. The trail then ascends more steeply with switchbacks reaching the cabin (closed) just below the firetower.

1 hour and 1.4 miles round trip. Elevation gain: 420'
Approach: In Norwich village, drive north on Main Street about half a mile to Turnpike Road. Turn left onto Turnpike Road and continue for 4.6 miles (pavement ends after 1.9 miles) to the trailhead parking area on the left.

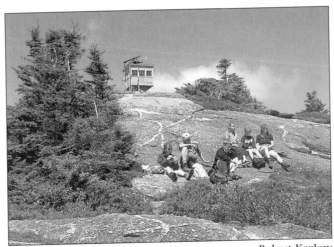

Mount Cardigan summit   Robert Kozlow

Mount Cardigan 3,121' (New Hampshire)

Although a low mountain, Cardigan's bare, rocky summit gives the feel of a higher peak. It is one of the classic mountains of New Hampshire and very popular with kids. From the picnic area, follow the **West Ridge Trail**. It ascends at an easy angle and the upper portion runs across bare ledges. You soon reach the open summit area with its panoramic views. The firetower is manned, and it is possible to visit with the ranger and learn about the mountain and its history. Descend by the same route.

2 hours and 3 miles round trip. Elevation gain: 1,220'

Approach: From Canaan (take exit 17 off I-89 to Enfield) on Route 4, continue 0.5 mile north on Route 118. Turn right, follow signs, and continue through Orange to Cardigan State Park and the trailhead.

Hikes almost in Vermont

While this book is about hiking the state's best day hikes, it seems useful to briefly discuss a few of the excellent day hikes that are very accessible from Vermont, because in some cases, just-across-the-border hikes are the closest, if not the best local option for Vermont-based hikers. New Hampshire's Mt. Wantastiquet for Brattleboro and Massachusetts' Mt. Greylock for Bennington are examples of this phenomenon. Mount Cardigan, described on the previous page, is another. The following is a brief overview of some outstanding hikes easily managed from Vermont:

For hikers originating in the Lake Champlain area (Burlington-Shelburne-Middlebury) some of the eastern Adirondack classics are easily accessed as day hikes:

Noonmark (3,556') in Keene Valley, 45 minutes from Essex, NY (take the Charlotte-Essex ferry) offers a 3-4 hour r/t, 5-mile hike with a vertical gain of 2,300'.

The Brothers, also in Keene Valley, is a 1-3 hour hike, depending on how high you go. 5 miles, 1,800' vertical.

Cascade Mountain (4,098') is about an hour from Essex, NY (ferry from Vermont). The view of the Adirondack High Peaks from its open summit is one of the best in Northeast. 4 hours, 4.8 miles, 2,000' vertical.

For those based in the Upper Connecticut Valley (Bradford-Norwich-White River Junction), the western edge of New Hampshire's White Mountains are tempting:

Moosilauke (4,802') about an hour from Bradford. 4-5 hours, 7 miles r/t, 2,500' vertical gain

Franconia Ridge Traverse, located about 1-1.5 hour drive from the Vermont border. This is a great classic of New England: the loop hike is 9 miles, with about 3,900' of climbing. Figure on 6-8 hours.

9 Manchester and Stratton Mountain

Manchester lies in the narrow valley formed by the Taconic Range to the west and the Green Mountains to the east. In this area most of the mountain hiking is linked to the Long Trail, with the Taconics seeing less activity. However, impressive Mount Equinox, which looms over Manchester to the west, is perhaps the area's best climb, while a paved toll road to the top provides access to the summit trails.

66 Mt. Equinox 3,840'

Mount Equinox rises almost 3,000' above Manchester and is the dominant mountain of the area. The **Blue Summit Trail** ascends the mountain, from Manchester Village. From the trailhead kiosk on West Union Street, take the **Red Gate Trail** to connect with the Blue Summit Trail. Here head left and continue along the woods road. The Red Gate Trail coincides with Blue Summit Trail for about a quarter of a mile before branching off left. After crossing the **Trillium Trail** and the **Maidenhair Trail**, Blue Summit Trail continues to the end of the road, at about 1.5 miles. Beyond here, the trail settles in for a steep climb up the flank of Equinox, gaining its southeast-running ridge at about 2 miles. Once on the ridge, the trail is less steep. At about 2.7 miles, you reach the intersection with the **Yellow Trail**. The Yellow Trail heads north (right) for 0.5 mile over relatively easy terrain to **Lookout Rock**, where there are excellent views across to the Bromley–Stratton area and Manchester in the valley below. From here, take **Lookout Rock Trail** on to the summit and the **Skyline Inn** (upper end of the Equinox Skyline Drive, a toll road). To descend, take Lookout Rock Trail for 0.1 mile then turn right on the Blue Summit Trail and take it back down.

Mt. Equinox from Manchester Center   Jared Gange

5–6 hours and 5.8 miles round trip. Gain: 2,750'
Approach: From Manchester Ctr., take Route 7A south
a mile to Manchester Village. Turn right on Seminary St.,
pass Burr and Burton Academy, and right onto West Union
St. The trailhead parking lot is up the hill on the right.

Equinox Preservation Trust

Most of the trail network on Mt. Equinox, including the
Blue Summit Trail and the other trails mentioned above,
is part of the Equinox Preserve, which is managed by the
Equinox Preservation Trust. The Preserve—encompassing
over 900 acres and about 11 miles of trail—is owned by
the Equinox Spa and Resort in Manchester. A free map of
the Preserve shows the hiking trails and provides information about the ecology of the area. The Preserve is open to
the public year-round for non-motorized recreational use.

Maps: *Vermont's Long Trail (GMC); Trail Map & Guide (Equinox
Preservation Trust); Manchester and the Mountains Hiking Map*

67 Prospect Rock 2,179'

A favorite short hike, Prospect Rock offers great views of Manchester, Mount Equinox, and to the north, Dorset Peak. From the gate at the end of the public road, start up the steep and rocky roadway (Old Rootville Road) and continue for about 1.5 miles to the **Long Trail**. The spur trail to Prospect Rock is about 120' farther south on the Long Trail, on your right. Return by the way you came.

2.5 hours and 3 miles round trip. Elevation gain: 1,000'

Approach: Drive east from Manchester Center (on Routes 11/30), turning right on East Manchester Road then left on Rootville Road. Limited parking at the end of the road.

68 Stratton Mountain 3,936'

The conventional hiking route up Stratton is from the south, via the **Long Trail**, although climbing the mountain from the ski area (north side) also is recommended. The fire tower on the top of Stratton Mountain, 0.8 mile south of the top of the ski area (Stratton's North Peak), provides a panoramic view extending to five states. From the parking area on Kelley Stand Road, follow the LT/LT north for 3.3 miles to the tower. From the summit, the LT/AT descends (left) 2.6 miles to secluded, but popular **Stratton Pond**, an important stopover with LT/AT thru-hikers. There are several shelters here, and during hiking season, GMC caretakers are in residence. Return to the car via the gradually descending 3.7-mile **Stratton Pond Trail** (blue blazes), which ends on Kelley Stand Road, a mile west of your starting point.

7-8 hours and 11 miles round trip. Gain: 1,910'

Approach: From the village of Stratton, drive west on the Arlington–West Wardsboro Road (Kelley Stand Road) to the Long Trail parking area.

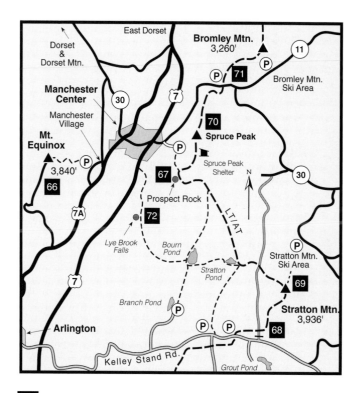

69 Stratton Mountain via ski trails

From the base of the ski area, bear right through the little ski village to the base of the gondola. The hike up the open ski trails runs to the north summit (ca. 3,885') and will take about an hour to an hour and a half. It is 0.7 mile (about 20 minutes) over to the higher south summit with its observation tower. Note that the lift runs during the summer season, so it is possible to ride up or down—or both!

70 Spruce Peak 2,080'

A popular hike over generally easy terrain, this trail gains only 240' in elevation from the highway. Head south on the LT/AT. There are a couple of viewpoints along the way, and from the short spur trail (right) on Spruce Peak, there is a good view to the west of Mount Equinox and the valley below. Return by the same route. **Spruce Peak Shelter**, one of the nicer cabins on the LT, lies 0.5 mile farther south and is at a somewhat higher elevation than Spruce Peak.

2.5 hours and 4.5 miles round trip. Elevation gain: 240'
Approach: From Manchester Ctr., drive east 5 miles on Routes 11/30 to the Long Trail highway crossing.

71 Bromley Mountain 3,260'

Hike north on the Long Trail/Appalachian Trail over generally moderate terrain to reach the top of Bromley, where there is a cafeteria and a good observation deck. The views south to Stratton Ski Area and of the other nearby mountains are excellent. Descend by the same route, or, as an alternative to trail walking, hike down the steep, grassy ski trails to the base of the Bromley ski area. (Arrange a car shuttle.)

4 hours and 5.6 miles round trip. Elevation gain: 1,460'
Approach: From Manchester Center, drive east on Routes 11 and 30 for 5 miles to the large parking area on the left, which is where the Long Trail crosses the highway.

Similar to Stratton Mountain, the ski runs at Bromley offer a great route up the mountain. As you climb the open, grassy slopes, the views just get better and better. From the base of the ski area, on Route 11, just east of the junction of Routes 11 and 30, follow lifts and ski trails to the top.

Lye Brook Falls   Lisa Densmore

72 Lye Brook Falls

Lye Brook Falls is one of the highest waterfalls/cascades in
Vermont. From the parking area, take the **Lye Brook Trail**
south (marked with blue blazes) for about 2 miles until it
crosses an old railroad bed. Here, head right on the railroad
bed for 0.3 mile to the falls. Return by the same route.

2.5 hours and 4 miles round trip. Elevation gain: 1,000'
Approach: From Route 11/30, east of Manchester Center,
turn right onto Richville Road, then left on East Manchester
Road. After the underpass, head right on Glen Road; at the
fork, bear right for another 0.5 of a mile to the trailhead
parking at the end of the road.

73 Griffith Lake and Baker Peak 2,850'

Although well below treeline, Baker has a rocky, partially exposed summit with a sweeping westerly view from Equinox in the south to Dorset Peak and many miles to the north. Take the **Lake Trail** (moderately steep) reaching **Baker Peak Trail** at 2 miles, after crossing McGinn Brook. After a mile of mostly easy walking (a few steep parts), you reach the **Long Trail**. Head left (north) on the LT for 0.1 mile to the top. Descend either by the same route or head south on the LT (easy terrain) for 1.9 miles to lovely **Griffith Lake**. From the lake, backtrack on the LT to the Lake Trail and the car.

Loop: 5–6 hours, 9 miles round trip. Gain: 2,350'

Approach: From Manchester, drive north on Route 7, 2.4 miles past Emerald Lake to Town Highway 5. Turn right and park on the left after 0.5 mile.

74 Little Rock Pond 1,850'

An easy hike takes you to a pretty pond nestled in a forested mountain setting. The well-used shelters and platforms in the vicinity attest to the area's popularity! Follow the LT (AT, too) north over easy terrain for 2 miles to reach the pond. A variation (longer) to the overlook on Green Mtn. (2,509') gives you the much-photographed view of the pond below. It is worth the extra effort: Continue past the southern end of the pond to **Green Mountain Trail**, then head left about 30 minutes. Return by the same route or continue on this trail back to Mount Tabor Road. The longer variations total 6 or 7.5 miles respectively.

2 hours, 4-5 miles round trip. Elevation gain: 350'

Approach: From Manchester Ctr., take Rt. 7 north to Danby. Turn right on FS #10 (Mt. Tabor Road) and continue to the Appalachian Trail/Long Trail crossing.

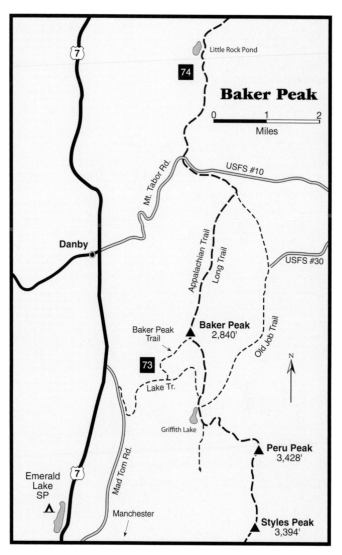

The Long Trail in early spring   Jared Gange

Appalachian Trail & Long Trail

The 2,100-mile Appalachian Trail is the premier long-distance hiking trail in the United States. Starting in Georgia, the "AT" runs along the crest of the Appalachian Range, eventually reaching Vermont's Green Mountains, before continuing to the White Mountains of New Hampshire and on into Maine. Vermont's own long-distance trail, the 270-mile Long Trail, runs the length of the state from south to north. These two trails coincide for about 100 miles in southern Vermont. Thus from the VT-Mass. border, near Bennington, all the way north to Killington Peak, the AT and the Long Trail are one and the same. Just north of Killington the AT branches east toward New Hampshire.

The Long Trail predates the Appalachian Trail and was the inspiration for it. Hiking the Long Trail is no walk in the park, as it has many steep and rough sections. But this is its charm and appeal: wild beauty and an untamed quality. While many choose to hike it in one continuous push—this usually takes about three weeks—probably the preferred approach is to "section hike" the trail, piece by piece, over a period of time, often years. Highways cross the trail at convenient intervals, making this latter alternative feasible. The many shelters and campsites along the route provide ample overnight spots. As designated by Vermont's legislature, the Green Mountain Club is the official steward and "protector" of the Long Trail. Its main mission, accordingly, is to secure a permanent corridor of land for the Long Trail, thus making it available for generations to come.

Rime ice   Jared Gange

75 Mount Antone 2,620'

Great views of the Dorset area await you at the top of Antone. The unblazed trail begins on Old Towne Road and continues past a fork (stay right) and a couple of intersections. Expect pleasant views of the Adirondacks along this road. At a well-marked junction, the Mount Antone road heads off to the right. Follow this road south—past an overnight shelter—and climb steeply up to the ridge top. Stay on the Mount Antone road as it descends, intersects with several roads, and finally ascends to the summit. From the summit a spur trail bends downward, offering great views of the nearby Adirondacks in New York.

3.5 hours, 5 miles round trip. Elevation gain: 890'

Approach: From the junction of VT 315 and VT 30 in East Rupert drive west on VT 315 for 2.4 miles to the Merck Forest sign on the left. Turn left on to the dirt road and continue to a gate and a 10-car parking area at 2.9 miles.

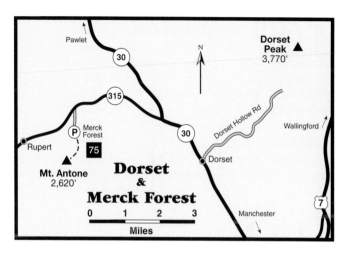

Dorset Peak 3,770'

The trail up this attractive, steep-sided (but viewless) peak is not maintained; however, it is climbed regularly. Dorset Peak is one of New England's 100 highest peaks and is a requirement for those on that particular quest. Similar in appearance to Equinox, it is very prominent from Route 7 when approaching from the north. The first mile of the route is negotiable with a 4-wheel drive vehicle. From a logging clearing, the trail ascends steeply past a hunting camp and continues to the saddle west of the summit before contouring around to the north. This trip is recommended only for hikers who are very experienced with route finding.

4 hours and 7 miles round trip. Elevation gain: 2,300'

Approach: From Dorset (west of Manchester Center), follow Dorset Hollow Rd., then Tower Rd. to the end of the valley, about 4 miles from Dorset. The trailhead is unmarked.

10 Bennington Area

Bennington is in the southwestern corner of the state, only 11 miles from Massachusetts. The main ridge of the Green Mountains lies a few miles to the east, while the Taconic Range is immediately to the west along the New York border. We describe several Bennington favorites as well as three hikes approached from Massachusetts. Two of them, Mount Greylock (3,491'), and Pine Cobble are *in* Massachusetts. The Greylock-Williamstown area has a well-developed trail network and its proximity to Bennington makes it worth visiting.

76 Harmon Hill 2,320'

Harmon Hill is a popular Bennington hike, giving good, close views of the town and the nearby Taconic mountains. The Forest Service keeps the summit area clear of brush by annual, controlled burns. From the parking on Route 9, head south on the **Long Trail**, at times quite steeply, reaching the top of Harmon Hill at about 1.7 miles. The steep sections of the trail use rock and log steps. Return by the same route.

2.5 hours and 3.4 miles round trip. Gain: 1,265'

Approach: From Bennington, drive east on Route 9 for 5 miles to the Long Trail crossing and the trailhead parking.

77 Bald Mountain 2,857'

The 7-mile **Bald Mtn. Trail** starts on North Branch Street in Bennington and traverses Bald Mountain, ending in Woodford Hollow, on the east side of the mountain. The shorter option is from the Woodford side. From your car, follow the blue-blazed trail first along old road beds, then up through a series of switchbacks, reaching the **West Ridge Trail** at 2.5 miles. Head right (north) for 0.1 mile to reach the top. Various points near the summit offer good views of Bennington and the nearby mountains. Return by the same route. The West Ridge Trail continues north, then east, for 7.6 miles to meet the Long Trail near Goddard Shelter on Glastenbury Mountain. See the loop hike described below.

4 hours and 5.2 miles round trip. Elevation gain: 1,600'
Approach: From Bennington, drive east 4 miles on Route 9 to the Woodford church. Head left on a gravel road for 0.8 mile to the trailhead, at a concrete water tank.

Pink Lady Slipper   John Gange

78 Glastenbury Mountain 3,747'

From Route 9, hike north on the Long Trail (and AT), most of the time in dense woods, passing two outlooks along the way. Plan to overnight at **Goddard Shelter** (lean-to with room for 10 people), 9.8 miles from the car. The summit and observation tower are 0.3 mile beyond the shelter. The view is one of a huge forest expanse, with few signs of man's intrusion upon nature. Return the next day by the same route, or, more interestingly, by the **West Ridge Trail** over **Bald Mountain** and down to Woodford (see previous description). The Bald Mountain variation takes a little longer.

12–13 hours (2 days), 20-mile loop, Gain: 2,400'

Approach: From Bennington, drive 5 miles east on Route 9 to the trailhead parking area where the Long Trail crosses the highway.

79 The Dome 2,748'

From the trailhead, follow the **Dome Trail** for 2.9 miles to the summit of Dome. At 1.5 miles, the **Agawon Trail** comes in from the right. The final half mile of the trail is rocky and interesting, and from the exposed rocks on the summit, there are good views of Mount Greylock, the Berkshires, the Taconics, and southern Vermont. The Dome Trail, blazed in orange, is maintained by Williams Outing Club at Williams College. The Dome is in Vermont, but the approach is from Massachusetts.

3.5 hours and 5.8 miles round trip. Elevation gain: 1,700'

Approach: From Route 7, 1.5 miles south of the Vt.-Mass. border, turn left (east) on Sand Springs Road. At White Oaks Road, turn left; park after 1.5 miles, 0.3 mile back inside Vermont.

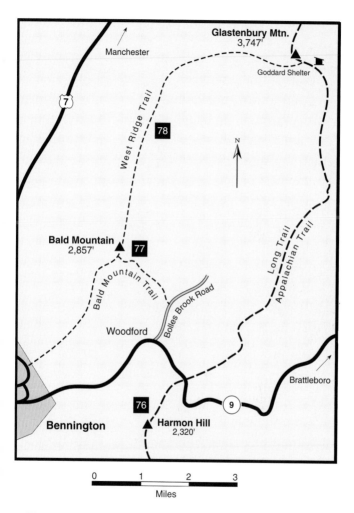

Maps: *Vermont's Long Trail (GMC); Green Mountain National Forest–South (National Geographic)*

Key to Color Photographs

1. Camel's Hump from Wind Gap,
   just off the Dean Trail   Matt Larson

2. High on Mt. Mansfield's Maple Ridge   Jared Gange

3. Summit ridge on Mt. Mansfield,
   just south of the top   Jared Gange

4. Hellbrook Trail, Mt. Mansfield   Jared Gange

5a. Smugglers Notch from the Stowe side   Jared Gange

5b. Butler Lodge, Mt. Mansfield   Jared Gange

6. Skylight Pond, near Middlebury Gap   Matt Larson

7. Mt. Philo, looking south
   over Lake Champlain   Jared Gange

8. Lake Willoughby and Mt. Pisgah   John Hadden

9. Lake of the Clouds, Mt. Mansfield   Matt Larson

10. View south from Mt. Hunger   Matt Larson

11. Smugglers Notch   Matt Larson

12. The Chin, Mt. Mansfield, from the north   Matt Larson

13. Camel's Hump from Huntington   John Hadden

14. Catamount Trail, Bolton to Trapp's   Jim Fredericks

15. Beaver Meadow and Whiteface Mtn.   Jared Gange

16. On a ski traverse of Camel's Hump   Jared Gange

1

4

Mount Greylock 3,491' (Massachusetts)

The highest mountain in the state, Greylock is an impressive sight. It is graced with many hiking trails, including the Appalachian Trail. Popular **Bascom Lodge**, on the top, is an important milestone for AT thru-hikers. The **Hopper Trail**, perhaps the classic route, climbs steeply up the north flank of the Hopper, a huge ravine on the west side. From the parking area, walk first along easy terrain before bearing right and climbing, reaching Sperry Rd. after about an hour (2 miles). The route then merges with Deer Hill Trail, passing Rockwell Rd. twice before meeting the AT (white blazes). Follow this to the summit. Return by the same route.

5 hours and 8.2 miles round trip. Elevation gain: 2,340'
Approach: From Williamstown (14 miles south of Bennington on Rte. 7), drive east on Rt. 2 for a short distance before turning right onto Water St. Continue south for 2.6 miles then turn left on Hopper Road; follow this 2.7 miles to the parking area.

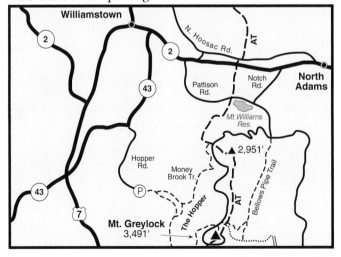

11 | Brattleboro & Mount Snow

In this chapter we present six hikes in the southeastern corner of the state and two in New Hampshire. Mount Olga, Mt. Snow, and Haystack Mtn. are near Wilmington, while Bald Mt. enjoys relative isolation in Townshend State Park, northwest of Brattleboro, off Route 30. Putney Mtn. and The Pinnacle lie just west of Putney. Mt. Wantastiquet, just across the river from Brattleboro, along with fabled Mt. Monadnock, east of Keene, complete the chapter.

80 Mount Snow 3,556'

Mt. Snow is the home of a large alpine ski area, which in the summer is a major mountain biking center. Generally not as steep as many other alpine areas, Mount Snow is excellent mountain biking terrain. Climb the mountain by the ski trails, which offer hiking on open, grassy slopes. From the rocky summit, there are extensive views of southern Vermont and Massachusetts, and New Hampshire's Mount Monadnock is picked out easily. There is an excellent view of nearby Somerset Reservoir. The gondola runs during the summer, giving the option of riding up and walking down.

2.5 hours and 3 miles round trip. Elevation gain: 1,500'
Approach: From Wilmington, drive north on Route 100 to Mount Snow. Park at the ski area base lodge.

The **Deerfield Trail** connects the top of Mt. Snow with the top of Haystack Ski Area. Primarily a cross country ski and snowmobile trail, this 3-mile trail segment is negotiable in summer but is quite rough and therefore something for more experienced and self-sufficient hikers.

Summit of the Pinnacle, Mt. Snow in the distance   J. Gange

81 Haystack Mountain 3,420'

Haystack Mountain is one of the more popular and interesting mountain hikes in southeastern Vermont. It is a satellite of Mount Snow, but for hikers Haystack has more significance. From the summit, there is a good view of **Haystack Pond** about 500' below. Many of the mountains of southern Vermont can be seen, and Mount Greylock in western Massachusetts, is also visible. Once the trailhead is located, the blue-blazed trail is easy to follow. Carefully note trail intersections on the way up for your return trip.

3 hours and 4.8 miles. Elevation gain: 1,030'

Approach: From Wilmington, drive west on Rt. 9 for 1.1 miles and turn right on Haystack Rd. Continue on Haystack, staying right, to Chimney Hill Rd. at about 1.2 miles. Turn left here, then right on Binney Brook Rd. At 2.6 miles from Rt. 9, reach the trailhead on the right.

Leave No Trace

Leave No Trace is both a slogan and a nonprofit organization. The organization seeks to promote sustainable practices for outdoor recreation so that future visitors' experiences are in no way reduced by earlier visitors. As such, it is a liaison between government agencies, like the Forest Service and the private sector to convey a message of healthy stewardship and sustainable use. A set of seven guidelines has been established.

1. Plan ahead and prepare
Plan your route and allow enough time. Make sure everyone in your group has the necessary food, water, equipment and clothing.

2. Camp on durable surfaces
Set up camp on packed ground or ledge, leaving the area as you found it. Keep groups below ten in number.

3. Minimize campfire impact
Campfires are discouraged; use a cook stove.

4. Dispose of waste properly
Bury human and dog waste at least 200 feet from water sources. Pack out all other waste.

5. Leave what you find
The mantra "take only photos, leave only footprints" is familiar to many. As is "carry out what you carry in". Thus picking flowers, removing plants or any natural objects is a no-no.

6. Respect wildlife
Observe rules regarding leashing of dogs, especially above tree line. Don't feed or chase wildlife.

7. Be considerate of other visitors
Use your common sense. For example, use a headset when playing music and minimize cellphone usage.

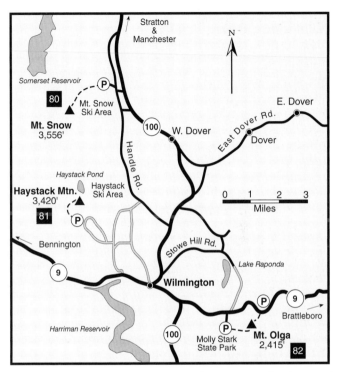

Maps: *Green Mountain National Forest–South (National Geographic); Vt. Atlas & Gazetteer, p. 21-23 (DeLorme)*

82 Mount Olga 2,415'

From the fire tower on Mount Olga's wooded summit there are sweeping views. The loop trail from **Molly Stark State Park** is blue-blazed and easy to follow. Mount Olga also can be climbed directly from Route 9, up the open ski trails (good views) of Hogback Ski Area. For those with less time, this alternative is shorter and offers less climbing.

Loop: 1.5 hours and 1.6 miles. Elevation gain: 500'

Approach: Mount Olga is located in Molly Stark State Park, 3.4 miles east of Wilmington, just south of Route 9. It is about 14 miles west of Brattleboro.

Map: A free hiker's map is available at the campground

83 Bald Mountain 1,680'

This modest mountain offers a good hike with a moderate climb. There are views of Bromley, Stratton, and the West River Valley from the summit. The trail starts from the campground, crossing and recrossing a brook before reaching the top after about 1.4 miles. The standard loop is done by descending the mountain via the steeper north side trail, which returns to the campground.

Loop: 2.5 hours and 2.8 miles. Elevation gain: 1,100'

Approach: From Townshend (20 miles from Brattleboro), drive west on Rt. 30. Cross the river at Townshend Dam and turn left back along the river (passing Vermont's longest single span covered bridge) to Townshend State Park.

Map: A free hiker's map is available at the campground.

Hiking with Dogs

While there is no doubt that a friendly, well-behaved dog is a wonderful hiking partner, people hiking with dogs need to be aware of the impact their pets can have on other hikers and the environment and act according.

When approaching other hikers, dog owners should have their dogs under their complete control. Most trail encounters are friendly, but for people uncomfortable with dogs, including many children, even a friendly nuzzle or face lick isn't a pleasant experience. It goes without saying that barking, growling, and jumping up should not be tolerated.

• It's considered a good idea to limit the number of dogs per hiking group to two.

• Some areas have special rules for dogs, ranging from a leash requirement to an outright ban. Some state parks require proof of rabies vaccination. Respect these requests.

• Always clean up after your dog, either by carrying out the dog poop or burying it well off (200 feet) the trail.

• Trails with ladders and cliffy sections can be very problematic and are best avoided. Cavorting in a stream is great fun, but avoid contaminating or muddying the water used by your fellow humans. Leash your dog near shelters.

• Make sure your dog is in shape for the outing you have planned. Just like us, dogs need conditioning. Build up gradually for those long hikes.

• Be sure to take adequate food and water for your canine companion.

• Dogs must be on leash above tree line, in alpine areas.

• Stay on the trail, and don't allow your dog to chase wild animals. Even an unsuccessful chase causes stress and is a threat to a wild animal's livelihood.

Putney Mountain - Windmill Hill Trails

The high ridge that runs north to south a few miles west of Putney village is called Windmill Mountain. Thanks to the efforts of the Putney Mountain Association and the Windmill Hill-Pinnacle Association there is now a well-marked, color-coded trail system along this ridge. At the southern end of the trail, Putney Mountain is only 0.6 mile from the trailhead. Its grassy, open hilltop is a popular viewing spot for hawk migrations. About 3 miles farther north along the ridge, the Pinnacle—the trail system's gem—offers sweeping views of the Green Mountains.

The gate at the Pinnacle trailhead J. Gange

84 The Pinnacle 1,684'

A combination of an old woods road, moderate grades and smooth dirt paths makes for a great walking or running experience. From the gate—a funky welded iron and stone creation—follow the red-marked **Holden Trail** (woods road) as it ascends over easy ground (bear right at the trail

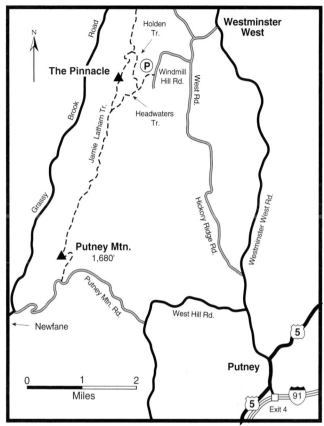

junction after 0.5 mile) to the **Jamie Latham Trail**. Head left to the summit clearing with its fine cabin, open on one side, and expansive westerly views including Haystack, Mt. Snow, Stratton and Bromley. (See photo page 123.) Either return by the same route (1.4 miles) or continue south for 1.2 miles on the Jamie Latham Trail to the blue-blazed **Headwaters Trail**. Head left and descend to the intersection

with the Holden Trail, closing the loop, and continue back
to your car.

3 hours, 5-mile loop, 600' of climbing

Approach: From the village of Westminster West, take
West Road for 1.0 mile to Windmill Hill Road North.
Follow it uphill, continuing a little over a mile to the
parking area / trailhead on the right. Westminster West is
located north of Putney and west of Westminster.

Maps: *Excellent hiking maps are available from Windmill Hill-
Pinnacle Association at www.windmillhillpinnacle.org.*

Use of Windmill Ridge Nature Reserve

Dogs are allowed on the trails, but they must be leashed.
Horses and mountain bikes are allowed, but not when
trails are soft or muddy, for example during late spring.
A cabin is available for overnight use: contact the Windmill
Hill-Pinnacle Association.

The Connecticut River from Mt. Wantastiquet   J. Gange

Mt. Wantastiquet 1,351' (New Hampshire)

For walking, mountain biking and mountain running, the carriage road up Mt. Wantastiquet is a fine workout. From the parking area, choose the upper gated road. A brisk 40-minute walk on this moderately graded gravel road (at times rocky) through nine switchbacks brings you to a fine lookout (right) over Brattleboro and the Connecticut River. Just beyond the lookout (near the tower), a rough footpath leads left (20 min.) to the top of a surprisingly big cliff of white marble with its sweeping southerly views.

2 hours and 3 miles roundtrip. Gain 1,200' (to lookout)
Approach: From Brattleboro, cross the river into NH and take the left immediately after the (second) bridge. Park on the right after 0.2 mile.

Mt. Monadnock 3,165' (New Hampshire)

Mt. Monadnock is one of the great classic hikes of New England, and its proximity to Brattleboro qualifies it as a "local" hike. The hike given here, the **Marlboro Trail**, starts out with easy grades but steepens, alternating between forest pockets and open rock ledges. About a half mile from the top, the summit area comes into view, and the Dublin Trail enters from the left. The upper mountain is a fantastic expanse of bare rock, the result of fires deliberately set by farmers many years ago to drive wolves from the area. Descend by the same route.

3¼ hours and 4.4 miles. Elevation gain: 1,865'
Approach: Thirty-five miles from Brattleboro, and well inside New Hampshire, Mount Monadnock draws hikers from southern Vermont. From NH Route 124, five miles east of the town of Marlboro, head left 0.7 miles on Shaker Farm Rd. to the trailhead.

12 | Groton State Forest

This popular recreation area is located east of Montpelier. It is heavily forested, but the numerous lakes and some interesting rock outcrops make it an area worth exploring. The state park (within the state forest) has several campgrounds and a network of hiking trails as well as other recreation possibilities. There is a day usage fee, but a free trail guide and map is available at the park entrance.

Approach: From Barre, take Route 302 east to Route 232, turn left, and drive past Lake Groton to Groton State Park.

85 Owl's Head 1,958'

This is a popular hike with great views of Lake Groton and beautiful Kettle Pond. On the top, trails on smooth granite bedrock radiate in all directions through spruces and blueberry bushes. The hiking trail begins off the road to **Osmore Pond**, and after avoiding a swampy area, climbs up to a parking area. It is then a steep 0.1 mile to the top.

1.5 hours and 3 miles round trip. Elevation gain: 230'
Approach: From New Discovery Campground B, follow signs to the trail. *Note:* The easy way to "hike" Owl's Head is to drive up the gravel road, which goes to within 0.1 mile of the actual summit.

86 Big Deer Mountain 1,992'

Big Deer is similar to Owl's Head but offers a slightly higher and less-visited summit with excellent views of nearby lakes and surrounding mountains. The first mile of the **Big Deer Mountain Trail** is quite easy, with the last half mile climbing steeply up to the summit area. The trail has blue blazes.

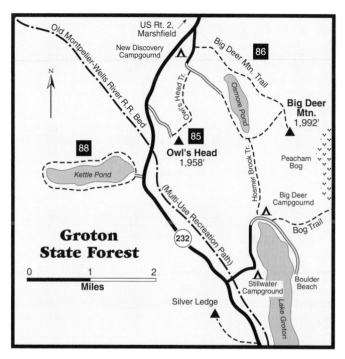

2 hours and 3.4 miles round trip. Elevation gain: 250'
Approach: Drive through the park entrance to where Campground B begins and turn left on the road to **Peacham Pond** for 0.3 mile. The trailhead is on the right with limited parking.

Maps: *Vt. Atlas & Gazetteer, p. 41 (DeLorme); and State Park map*

87 Spruce Mountain 3,037'

Located at the western edge of Groton State Forest, only the summit of Spruce is in the Forest, and the mountain is some distance away from Lake Groton. From the gate, follow the woods road to the right, staying on it for about a mile as it swings to the south side of the mountain. At 1.5 miles, the trail begins a more or less steady climb to the top, at times passing across exposed granite. From the tower on the summit, there are excellent views in all directions. Descend by the same route. Nearby **Signal Mountain**, (3,348') is the highest in this range, but has no trail to the summit.

3 hours, 4.4 miles round trip. Elevation gain: 1,340'

Approach: From the main intersection in downtown Barre, head east on US 302, passing through the round-about in East Barre at 3.7 miles: at 5 miles, turn left on Reservoir Rd. At 10.7 miles, bear right on East Hill Rd., and at 11.5 miles, right again onto Spruce Mountain Rd. Follow this to trailhead parking, 12.6 miles from Barre.

View of Owl's Head in Groton State Forest　　　　Vt. Dept. of FPR

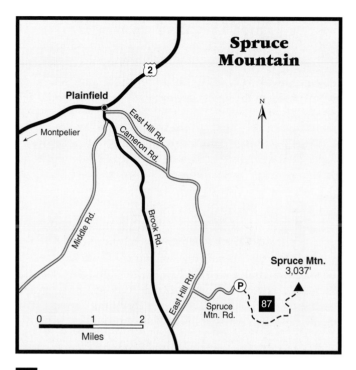

Spruce Mountain

2 (US)

Plainfield

Montpelier

East Hill Rd.

Cameron Rd.

Brook Rd.

Middle Rd.

East Hill Rd.

N

Spruce Mtn.
3,037'

P

87

Spruce
Mtn. Rd.

0   1   2
Miles

88 Kettle Pond Trail

This pleasant hike skirts the shoreline of a secluded pond. It takes an hour or two and is a good hike for families. The trail is somewhat rocky and wet at the far end of the pond. Starting from the highway, walk around the pond in a counter-clockwise fashion, ending at the Kettle Pond Group Camping Area just south of where you began the hike.

1-2 hours, 3-mile loop. Elevation gain: negligible
  Approach: Parking on the west side of the road, about a mile south of the side road up Owl's Head.

13 Northeast Kingdom

The cool deep waters of Lake Willoughby, a land-locked fjord, are a mecca for fishermen, while the cliffs of Mount Pisgah offer some of the best ice climbing in the Northeast. Although the summits are wooded and well below the treeline, the hikes in this region offer some of the most spectacular views in Vermont. Lake Willoughby is about 22 miles north of St. Johnsbury. Nearby Burke Mountain and more remote Mount Monadnock are also interesting.

89 Mount Pisgah 2,751'

Mount Pisgah is one of Vermont's more dramatic mountains, and the view of **Lake Willoughby** from the top of the 1,200' cliffs will not disappoint you. The popular **South Trail** leaves the highway and crosses a bog area on bridges. The trail then ascends very steeply, before passing perch-like **Pulpit Rock**, with its aerial view of the south end of the lake. The main trail is safe enough, but the mountainside is extremely steep—use caution! After another sustained climb, the gradient eases before reaching a rock slab with sweeping views to the south. The wooded summit is just beyond, at 1.7 miles, where a spur trail leads right to an interesting view of Bald Mtn. From the top, descend a short way (on North Trail) to reach the side trails to the stunning cliff-top lookouts. They are larger and safer than Pulpit Rock. Descend the way you came up.

2.5 hours, 3.5 miles. Elevation gain: 1,450'

Approach: From Lyndonville, take Route 5 north to West Burke then Route 5A for 6 miles to a parking area (left) just south of Lake Willoughby. The South Trail begins across the highway.

Mount Pisgah and Lake Willoughby   John Hadden

90 Mount Pisgah from the north

The popular 2.2-mile **North Trail** also starts from Route 5A, at a point 3 miles north of South Trail's trailhead. The path climbs on an old woods road, first at a moderate pitch then more steeply, until it reaches the junction with the trail to Long Pond. From here, the trail climbs less steeply and passes side trails (right) to North Lookout and West Lookout. The upper lookout offers the more impressive view of Lake Willoughby, 1,200' below. The North and South Trails meet at the wooded summit. Return by the same route.

2.5 hours, 3.5 miles. Elevation gain: 1,400'

Approach: From Lyndonville, take Route 5 to West Burke then Rt. 5A for 9 miles to roadside parking on the right side of the highway.

91 Mount Hor 2,648'

Mount Hor is directly across Lake Willoughby from Mount Pisgah, and its main attraction is the spectacular view of the lake and Pisgah's cliffs. The blue-blazed trail does not actually go to the top of Mt. Hor but does lead to several viewpoints. After 0.7 mile, the trail forks. Take the right fork another 0.7 mile to **East Lookout**, where there is a superb view of Mount Pisgah, and to **North Lookout**, with impressive views of the lake and north into Canada. The left fork climbs 0.3 mile to **Summit Lookout**, with good views to the west.

2 hours and 2.8 miles round trip. Elevation gain: 700'

Approach: Turn left (west) off Route 5A, about 6 miles north of West Burke and drive up a gravel road (the CCC Road) for 1.8 miles to a parking area on the right.

92 Wheeler Mountain 2,371'

This popular, short hike has the feel of a rock climb as you clamber up and across smooth granite slabs. After a short distance, the trail divides into the **Red Trail** (shorter, steeper) and the **White Trail**. They merge just below the top. Most hikers will enjoy the steeper ascent, followed by the slightly longer White Trail on the descent. After reaching the summit ledges, continue a few minutes to spectacular **Eagle Cliff** where there are better views towards Lake Willoughby and of the surrounding area. The clean granite slabs make this hike unusual for Vermont. A somewhat similar but longer hike is Maple Ridge on Mt. Mansfield.

2 hours and 2 miles round trip. Elevation gain: 700'

Approach: From Route 5, 8.3 miles north(west) of West Burke, turn right on to Wheeler Pond Road, and drive for 2 miles to a small signed parking area on the left.

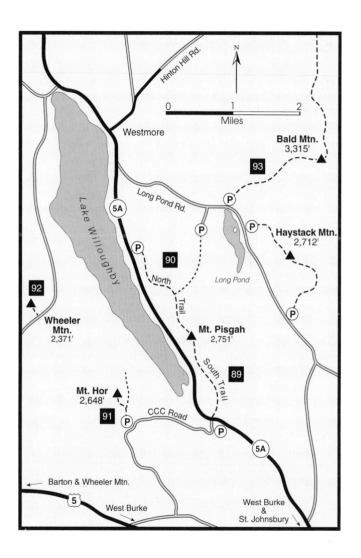

93 Bald Mountain 3,315'

With its summit tower, and as the highest mountain in the Lake Willoughby area, Bald Mtn. offers the best general views in the region. There are two routes to the summit (note map). The Long Pond route starts about 100 yards east of the pond access. Using various old woods roads, the trail ascends generally moderately to the summit with only limited views along the way. Descend by same trail.

3 hours and 4 miles round trip. Elevation gain: 1,450'

Approach: From Westmore (Lake Willoughby), drive 2 miles east on Long Pond Road to Long Pond and park at the lake access parking or just beyond, at the trailhead.

94 Burke Mountain 3,267'

Home of Burke Mountain Ski Area, Burke also offers good hiking and mountain biking. There is a road to the top (hiking is allowed, car toll), but the best hiking route begins as a small road to the right of the ski area parking lot. After 0.8 mile, take the red-blazed trail (left) and climb about 800' to the fire road. Here, at a lean-to, the trail divides, with the blue-blazed route taking a steeper line to the summit ridge. The two trails rejoin about 50 feet below the top of West Peak. Follow the **Profile Trail** to the summit tower, where there are excellent views of Mount Pisgah and nearby mountains. Descend by same route or by ski trails.

2.5 hours and 3.5 miles round trip. Gain: 1,270'

Approach: From East Burke (just north of Lyndonville), continue 1 mile on Mountain Road to the Burke Mountain Sherburne Lodge parking lots.

Maps: Northeast Kingdom Hiking Trail Map (GMC); Northern Vermont Hiking (Map Adventures)

95 Mount Monadnock 3,140'

Vermont's Mount Monadnock, in the extreme northeastern corner of the state, is a local landmark, rising over 2,000' above the Connecticut River. Although it is a fine hike, on a good trail, Monadnock is almost unknown to hikers outside the area. From the bridge, walk south along the highway about 100' and turn right on to a private road. This soon turns into a trail, and climbing steeply, crosses a stream (45 minutes) and continues to climb steeply before slackening and reaching the summit after about 2 hours. The trail is viewless until the top. Climb the tower to get above the trees for spectacular views of the North Country, into Canada, and of New Hampshire's Mt. Washington and the Presidential Range. Mt. Monadnock is only 10 feet lower than its southern cousin, Mt. Ascutney, another monadnock.

3.5 hours and 5 miles round trip. Elevation gain: 2,100'

Approach: Across the river from Colebrook, NH, Mount Monadnock is on Route 102, about 30 miles east of Island Pond. Park just south of the Route 26 bridge on Rt. 102.

View from Wheeler Mountain   Lisa Densmore

14 The Northern Frontier

The mountains traversed by the Long Trail from Route 15 north to Canada are sometimes referred to as the Northern Frontier. Although less visited than the terrain to the south, there is fine hiking in this wilder, more remote part of the state. A good deal of the Long Trail runs across private land, and the Green Mountain Club is working with landowners in the area to secure permanent protection for the Long Trail corridor. From the summit of Belvidere Mountain, it is only 27 miles via the Long Trail to the Canadian border.

96 Belvidere Mountain 3,360'

A fine, distinct mountain in an isolated setting, Belvidere offers a very worthwhile hike. On a windy day, the sensation from the 70' fire tower is like flying! The route follows the **Long Trail** north from Rt. 118 and offers pleasant walking on an interesting and varied trail. Although here in the more northern part of the state, the forest cover is lower and sparser than farther south, views still are limited until the top is reached. At Belvidere Saddle (3,200'), leave the Long Trail (right) and take the **Forester's Trail** the final 0.2 mile to the top. (Note that the Forester's Trail also descends from the saddle northeast to the asbestos mine access road, 4.5 miles north of Route 118.) From the top, it seems the whole of northern Vermont is on display.

4 hours and 5.6 miles round trip. Elevation gain: 2,140'
Approach: From Jeffersonville, drive north on Route 109, turn right on Route 118, and park where the Long Trail crosses the highway, near the height of land.

Firetower on Belvidere's summit   Jared Gange

Long Trail footbridge across the Lamoille River   Jared Gange

97 Prospect Rock 1,040'

This is an easy, popular hike a few miles west of the town of Johnson. From the Long Trail's crossing of Hogback Road, a short distance west of the Ithiel Falls Camp Meeting grounds, the LT starts off with easy grades that become somewhat steeper as the trail winds its way upward. The rock ledges on Prospect Rock give good views to the south of the Lamoille Valley below and the nearby hills. Return to your car by the same route.

1–1.5 hours, 1.5 miles, elevation gain: 530'

Approach: From Johnson, drive west 1.6 miles on Route 15 to Hogback Road. Bear right and continue about 0.9 miles to where the Long Trail crosses Hogback Rd. The foot bridge (shown at left) is just a minute south on the Long Trail.

Happy hikers on the summit!   Jared Gange

98 Laraway Mountain 2,790'

Laraway Mountain is the highest summit along the crest of the Green Mountains between Route 15 (near Johnson) and Route 118. From the parking area at the end of Codding Hollow Road, take the **Long Trail** north. There is a good viewpoint at 2 miles with a very interesting view of Mount Mansfield, 15 miles to the south. The summit is reached at 2.4 miles. Descend by the same route.

3.5 hours and 4.8 miles round trip. Elev. gain: 1,550'

Approach: From Jeffersonville, drive north on Rt. 118 to Codding Hollow Rd., about 1.5 miles past Waterville. Follow it to the end (2.7 miles), staying left at 1.4 miles.

99 Mount Norris 2,575'

The **Mount Norris Trail**, maintained by the Mount Norris Boy Scout Reservation, follows logging roads and creek beds as it winds through hardwood forest, picking up various views before culminating in marvelous vistas of Belvidere Mountain, Jay Peak, and the landscape to the east and south. As the trail steepens you will encounter rock outcroppings until you reach the enjoyable final stroll on the wide ridge that continues to the summit. The trail is marked with flagging tape. Return by the same route. Mount Norris lies to the east of the Long Trail and is not part of the Long Trail System.

2.5 hours and 3.6 miles, elevation gain: 1,300'

Approach: From Eden Mills, drive 2 miles north on Route 100. The trailhead is on the west side of the road, across from the Mt. Norris Boy Scout Reservation.

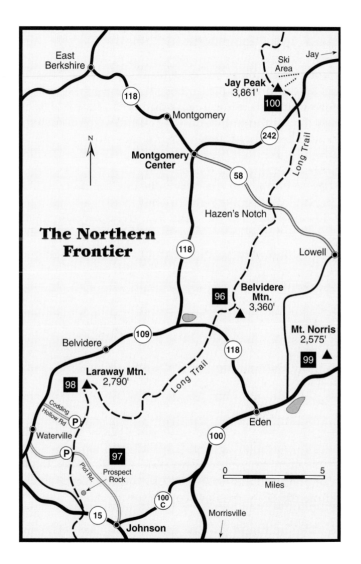

100 Jay Peak 3,861'

With a large tram station adjacent to the summit, Jay does not provide an unspoiled wilderness experience. However, this hike traverses a fine section of the **Long Trail**, and the views from the summit are superb. Take the Long Trail north from the parking area on Rt. 242. The rocky, well-maintained trail climbs briskly through birches and into the spruce-fir zone. Near the top, the trail crosses a ski trail before the final climb to the bare rock summit. Descend by the same route. It is also possible to climb Jay by one of the ski trails. The tram is in operation during the summer.

3 hours and 3.4 miles round trip. Elevation gain: 1,680'
Approach: From Montgomery Center, drive 6.8 miles north on Route 242 (or 5 miles south from the village of Jay) and park at the trail head parking, just south of the height of land.

Mt. Mansfield from the north   Jared Gange

Summit of Jay Peak   Lisa Densmore

Just to the south of Jay Peak, a 7-mile portion of the Long Trail makes for a good day hike. It is about 4 hours walking from Hazen's Notch to Route 242. From Hazen's Notch, head north on the Long Trail, passing Hazen's Notch Camp after a half mile, before beginning a steep climb. The summit of **Buchanan Mountain** (2,940') is reached at 4 miles, with a good view of Jay Peak. **Chet's Lookout** (at 4.2 miles) and **Domey's Dome** (at 5.2 miles) have good views as well. At 7 miles, the Long Trail crosses Route 242 and begins its ascent of Jay Peak. Montgomery Center is about 6.5 miles to the west by road. To reach Hazen's Notch, follow Hazen's Notch Road 5.5 miles from Montgomery Center.

Maps: *Vermont's Long Trail (GMC); Vt. Atlas & Gazetteer, p. 46, 52-53 (DeLorme)*

Vermont Youth Conservation Corps

Many of the trails featured in this guidebook have been built, restored, and maintained by the Vermont Youth Conservation Corps (VYCC). The VYCC is a statewide, year-round, nonprofit conservation and education organization with a mission to teach individuals to take personal responsibility for all their actions. Each year the VYCC enrolls over 300 young people, ages 16 to 24, to complete high-priority conservation, agriculture, and community service projects under the guidance of highly-trained adult leaders. Since 1985, the VYCC has served more than 5,400 young people from every county and nearly every town in Vermont.

Diversity is the hallmark of the VYCC experience. On any given crew, one finds youth from wealthy backgrounds working alongside those who are economically disadvantaged. Corps Members who find it difficult to read sit with students bound for Ivy League schools; each Corps Member brings a different set of past experiences and perspectives to the crew. In this environment, Corps Members learn to embrace diversity resulting in a tremendous amount of learning and personal growth.

A wide array of programs—a conservation program that employs hundreds of young people, work crews for the blind and visually impaired, farm internships, a school program for at-risk students, and all-female leadership crews—provide professional and academic opportunities to develop self confidence, to improve technical and leadership skills, and to gain work experience through the completion of projects firmly rooted in Vermont's traditions and landscape.

To identify and complete projects, VYCC crews regularly work with federal and state agencies, towns, and nonprofit trail organizations like the Appalachian Mountain Club, the Green Mountain Club, the Catamount Trail Association, and the Cross Vermont Trail Association. Typical work projects include the construction and maintenance of trails, managing Vermont State Parks, and restoring watershed health through invasive species removal and erosion control projects.

Corps members building a retaining wall   VYCC

15 | Multi-day Hikes on the Long Trail

Vermont's Long Trail, the 272-mile rugged footpath that runs along the ridgeline of the Green Mountains, from Massachusetts to Canada, is wonderful resource for both long-distance hikers and day hikers. Those planning on hiking the entire trail should figure on 3-4 weeks of walking. However, with over 180 miles of short, well-maintained side trails that access the Trail—making it relatively easy to reach all the favorite summits and other attractions—the Trail sees the vast majority of its use from day hikers. Many of the hikes described in this guide, including most of Vermont's "classic hikes" involve a combination of Long Trail and access trail.

In this chapter, we present three sections of the Long Trail that can be done either as 2-day hikes or as quite ambitious, strenuous 1-day hikes. The first one is a hike in the Manchester area, the climb of **Stratton Mountain**, down to popular **Stratton Pond**, and north on the LT/AT across Spruce Peak to Rt. 11/30, near Bromley Ski Area. The second is a challenging hike from **Appalachian Gap** (Mad River Valley) over **Camel's Hump** and down to the Winooski River, just a couple hundred feet above sea level. Lastly, we describe the section from VT 15 near Johnson south along the **Sterling Range** and across the top of Smugglers' Notch Ski Area, ending in **Smugglers' Notch**. In addition to these hikes, two other noteworthy sections of the trail are described in the main text as day hikes: the 10.7-mile stretch of the LT from Lincoln Gap to App Gap and a south to north traverse of the Mt. Mansfield ridge, starting from Lake Mansfield in Nebraska Valley and ending in Smugglers' Notch.

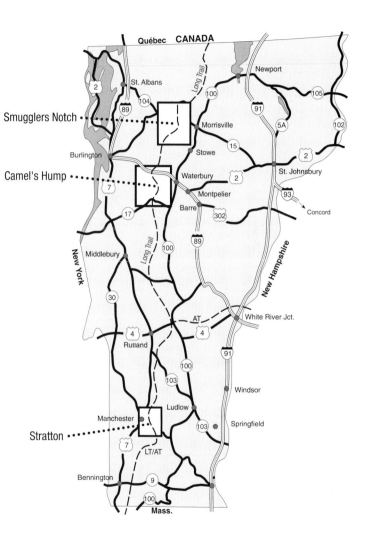

Smugglers Notch •••••••

Camel's Hump •••••

Stratton •••••••••

Kelley Stand Rd. to Rt. 11/30 (Stratton)

From Kelley Stand Road (Stratton-Arlington Rd.) heading north on the Long Trail (and Appalachian Trail) takes you up Stratton Mountain, then down to Stratton Pond before continuing north past Prospect Rock and Spruce Peak to Vermont Routes 11&30.

The LT/AT heads north from Kelley Stand Road initially over easy terrain, and after crossing the "IP" Road (International Paper) Road at 1.8 miles, commences a switch-backing climb, passing a viewpoint at about 2 miles. Continuing steeply, the trail passes through a saddle before reaching the south summit of **Stratton Mountain** at 3.8 miles. At 3,936', Stratton is Vermont's 7th highest peak. Climb the tower for a panoramic view of the Vermont and Massachusetts landscape. Stratton Mountain Ski Area is located on the north summit, about ¾ mile to the north.

The LT/AT now heads west off the summit towards **Stratton Pond**, reaching it after 3.2 miles. Just before the pond (0.1 mile), the **Stratton Pond Trail** comes in from the left. (It leads in 3.7 miles back to Kelley Stand Road.) To reach **Stratton Pond Shelter** head down Stratton Pond Trail 150', then right 300' on a side trail. There is space for 20 here.

Stratton Pond is an immensely popular spot and it is carefully managed by the GMC. Camping is allowed only at designated locations. There is additional camping space at the North Shore Tenting Area, just to the north.

Heading north from the pond you cross Winhall River at 8.9 miles (from Kelley Stand), and then after generally easy

Stratton Pond   Lisa Densmore

terrain pass Branch Pond Trail at 11.7 miles. (It is 0.5 mile south on this trail to **Douglas Shelter**, space for 10. From the above junction follow Old Rootville Road 0.9-mile to **Prospect Rock** (spur trail 150 feet to left) with its good views of the Manchester region. Note: Rootville Road continues down 1.8 miles to Manchester Center.

Now the Long Trail leaves Rootville Rd (right), and at 14.7 miles, brings you to the 0.1-mile spur trail west (left) to **Spruce Peak Shelter** (space for 16). At 15.1 miles, there is again a short spur trail west: to **Spruce Peak** with good views to the west. From here, continuing over varied terrain to the highway, the Long Trail reaches Vermont routes 11 and 30 at 17.5 miles. It is 5.8 miles west to Route 7A in Manchester Center.

Approach: The starting point is located on Stratton-Arlington Road, 3.4 miles from Stratton village at the Long Trail road crossing. Stratton village is about 11 miles south of Bondville (base of Stratton Mountain Ski Area), or 3.4 miles west of West Wardsboro.

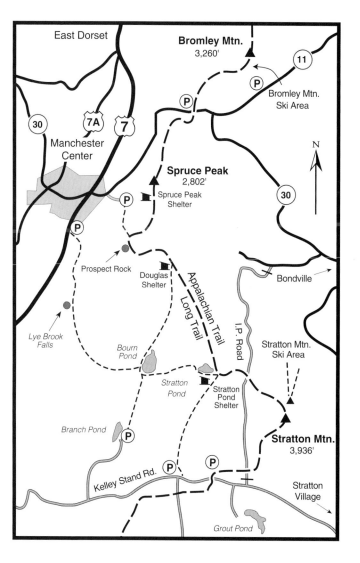

Appalachian Gap to the Winooski River

The Long Trail's 19-mile segment from Route 17 in Appalachian Gap ("App Gap") north to the Winooski River is the northern portion of the **Monroe Skyline**. In addition to a spectacular traverse of **Camel's Hump**, the Trail in this segment crosses Burnt Rock Mountain and descends almost 4,000' on magnificent Bamforth Ridge.

There are four shelters along the way, **Birch Glen Camp** at 2.6 miles, **Cowles Cove Shelter** at 5.5 miles, **Montclair Glen Lodge** at 10.6 miles, and north of Camel's Hump, **Bamforth Ridge Shelter** at 16 miles.

Heading north from App Gap, you reach a cliff top view of Camel's Hump at **Molly Stark's Balcony** after 1.3 miles. At 2.6 miles you come to Birch Glen Camp (space for 12) and 5.5 miles, Cowles Cove Shelter where there is bunk space for 8. From Birch Glen Camp, the **Beane Trail** descends in 1.5 miles to Carse Road in Huntington (Hanksville).

From Cowles Cove Shelter, the LT ascends moderately to Huntington Gap (the Catamount Ski Trail and a snowmobile trail cross the main ridge here) and continues along the ridge before making a steep climb up **Burnt Rock Mountain** (3,168'). This is popular hike during fall foliage: the views are excellent. Note: **Hedgehog Brook Trail**, a 2-mile side trail, accesses the Long Trail (from Fayston) joining it 0.6 mile south of Burnt Rock Mtn. (See Hike #37, page 68.)

From Burnt Rock Mtn., the trail ascends the summit pair **Ira Allen** and **Ethan Allen** (3,680') before dropping very steeply into **Wind Gap**. Here, **Montclair Glen Lodge** (fee, caretaker in

Montclair Glen Lodge   Jared Gange

season, space for 10), at 10.6 miles from App Gap, is a good spot to end your first day. Nearby, the Forestry Trail departs left (west) towards Huntington, and a little farther on, the Dean Trail heads right (east) down the Waterbury side to the Monroe Trail.

While it is only 5.4 miles from Montclair Glen Lodge to Bamforth Ridge Shelter (space for 9), to get there the LT runs up and over Camel's Hump, an arduous and spectacular trek. This section of the LT is perhaps the most alpine

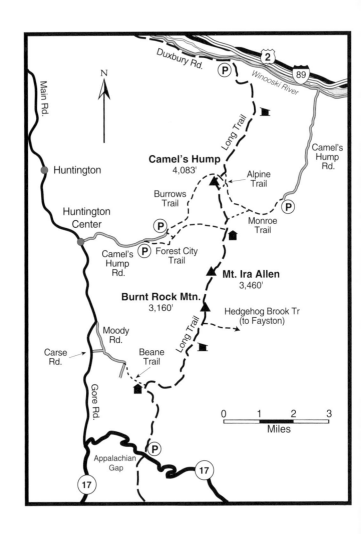

(steep, rocky and exposed) stretch of the entire Long Trail. From Wind Gap, the trail initially ascends very steeply; at times it's a scramble. There are excellent views along here. Then, after a relatively mellow, but slabby, section, you make the very steep, sustained climb to the base of the summit cliffs. Here contour left, ascend the final slabs, and reach the beautiful, open **summit of Camel's Hump** (4,083') at 12.5 miles from App Gap. From the summit, descend Camel's Hump's steep north shoulder, soon passing the Burrows (left) and Monroe (right) side trails in a small clearing. After 1.1 miles and 1,300' of descent from the summit, you pass the northern end of the Alpine Trail (right). Continue down the often rough, but always interesting (intermittent open areas, see photo page 57) Bamforth Ridge, reaching **Bamforth Ridge Shelter** (0.2-mile side trail right, space for 9) after a very tough 5.4 miles.

From here, more descending awaits. There are several good viewpoints and one very steep section before you reach the parking lot on River Road (Duxbury Road), at the Winooski River.

Approach: The Long Trail crosses Route 17 at Appalachian Gap. App Gap is 6 miles west of Waitsfield and 9.5 miles east of Route 116 (Hinesburg-Bristol highway). Parking is available just west of the trail crossing.

Route 15 south to Smugglers Notch

The Long Trail south from Route 15 to Smuggler's Notch provides an interesting and challenging 14-mile hike that can be done conveniently as a two-day trip, or as a more strenuous one-day effort.

From the trailhead parking at the Rail Trail on West Settlement Road, follow the white-blazed Long Trail (LT) past some additional parking areas. The trail traverses generally moderate terrain, reaching **Bear Hollow Shelter** (space for 12) at 3.3 miles.

From here, the trail climbs steadily and at times very steeply, before finally bringing you to the pointed summit of **Whiteface Mountain** (3,714') at 6.4 miles. The summit is wooded, but there are several excellent lookouts. Drop off the summit on a sharp, narrow ridge, reaching **Whiteface Shelter** (space for 5) after having walked just under 7 miles from the Rail Trail. Note: It's possible to exit here via a one-mile trail to Beaver Meadow Lodge. From there, it's 3 miles to Beaver Meadow Road/Mud City Loop.

Part two continues along the rugged summits of the **Sterling Range**. A mile from the shelter—after cresting **Morse Mountain** at 3,486'—you come to **Hagerman Overlook** with its interesting view of Mansfield. Drop into **Chilkoot Pass** (a side trail leads in 0.8 mile to Beaver Meadow Lodge) before making the steep climb to the summit of **Madonna Peak** (3,668'), part of the **Smugglers' Notch Ski Area**. There are sweeping views here of Mt. Mansfield and to the north.

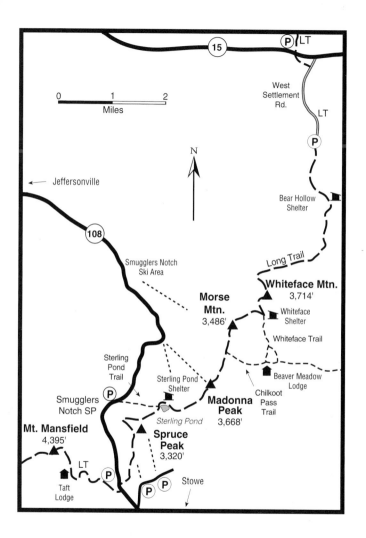

Continuing, another 1.2 miles brings you to **Sterling Pond Shelter** (space for 12), and 0.2 mile beyond, the attractive and popular area around the outlet of **Sterling Pond**. From here down to Route 108 on the Long Trail, and the end of the hike, it's another 3.4 miles. The LT passes close by the spectacular overlook (short spur trail right; use extreme caution!) into Smugglers' Notch from the top of **Elephant's Head,** before continuing its steady descent the road. Note: Hikers wanting a quicker exit to Route 108 can descend steep (but very popular) **Sterling Pond Trail** (1.1 miles) directly to Smugglers' Notch and Route 108. It leaves the LT (right), just 0.1 mile from the pond outlet.

Sterling Pond, looking toward Mt. Mansfield   Matt Larson

Madonna Peak and the Long Trail route   Jared Gange
as seen from Spruce Peak

Approach: The starting point is located at the junction of the Rail Trail and West Settlement Road, near Johnson. West Settlement Road is 2.3 miles west of Johnson on Route 15. Drive up West Settlement Rd. for 0.7 miles to the Rail Trail and parking. The end point of this Long Trail hike is at the roadside picnic area on Route 108, 8.4 miles from Stowe and Route 100.

• Outdoor Gear Exchange •

HOWEVER YOU'RE ENJOYING THE GREENS, OGE HAS YOUR MEANS!

HIKE   SKI   PADDLE

NOW WITH AN EXPANDED SELECTION
37 CHURCH STREET   BURLINGTON
LOCALLY OWNED SINCE 1995

KL MOUNTAIN SHOP.COM

VERMONT'S ONLINE OUTDOOR SPECIALISTS
2613 SHELBURNE RD, SHELBURNE VT / 877.284.3270
FREE ONE DAY LOCAL DELIVERY

patagonia   Marmot   MOUNTAIN HARD WEAR   THE NORTH FACE   Black Diamond

THE NORTH FACE STORE @
KL SPORT
210 COLLEGE ST/866.715.3223

VISIT THE NORTH FACE STORE IN BURLINGTON, VT

Preserve & Protect
Vermont's Hiking Trails

BECOME A
Green Mountain
Club Member

Through membership
dues and donations
The Green Mountain
Club maintains the
Long Trail System

www.GreenMountainClub.org
4711 Waterbury-Stowe Rd / (802) 244-7037
Visit us on Facebook or email gmc@greenmountainclub.org

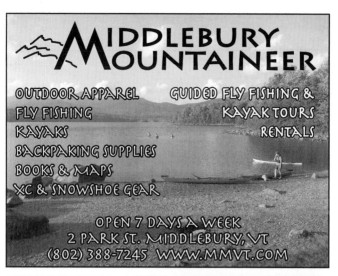

MIDDLEBURY MOUNTAINEER

OUTDOOR APPAREL
FLY FISHING
KAYAKS
BACKPAKING SUPPLIES
BOOKS & MAPS
XC & SNOWSHOE GEAR

GUIDED FLY FISHING &
KAYAK TOURS
RENTALS

OPEN 7 DAYS A WEEK
2 PARK ST. MIDDLEBURY, VT
(802) 388-7245 WWW.MMVT.COM

**Custom footbeds &
orthotics made on-site
for athletes, hikers, &
everyday victims of gravity**

THE
**MOUNTAIN
GOAT**

FINE OUTDOOR CLOTHING & GEAR
SINCE 1987

**4886 Historic Main St.
Manchester Center, VT
802-362-5159
Mon-Sat 10-6
Sun 11-5
mountaingoat.com**

H.E. Shaw Company

Main Street
Stowe, Vermont
802-253-4040
www.heshaw.com

**Helping Vermonters
and visitors survive in
style since 1895**

*Hiking Boots, Casual Footwear,
Trail Running Shoes,
Expert Bootfitting,
Hiking Accessories & Maps*

*Featuring Asolo, Merrell, Keen,
Patagonia, North Face, Woolrich,
Royal Robbins and Horny Toad*

Clothing for every kind of Yankee weather
Over 20,000 pairs of boots & shoes in stock
Camping, hunting saddlery, kayaks, snowshoes

Open 8:30-5:30 Friday till 8PM closed Sunday
Bradford, Vermont • (800) 222-9316

SUPPORT

VERMONT YOUTH CONSERVATION CORPS

1949 East Main Street, Richmond, Vermont 05477
800.639.8922 • info@vycc.org • www.vycc.org
Find us on Facebook.

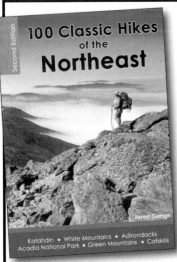

**Guide to the
best mountain
hikes of the
northeastern U.S.**

- Adirondacks
- Catskills
- White Mountains &
  Mount Washington
- Green Mountains
- Acadia National Park
  & Katahdin
- 2nd edition

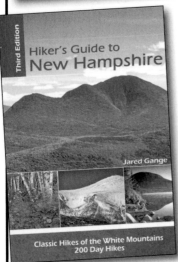

**New Hampshire
Hiking Guide**

- The 4,000-footers
- AMC huts and the AT
- 200 hikes
- 50 photos & 30 maps
- Winter hikes
- Hikes with children
- 3rd edition

From Huntington Graphics

The
Catamount Trail
300 Miles of Backcountry Skiing the Length of Vermont

Winter Adventure at its Best!

Join Now!
www.CatamountTrail.org

16 Backcountry Skiing

With the rediscovery of the telemark turn and today's excellent equipment, skiers are able to handle most terrain. Hiking trails (on Camel's Hump, for example) are often used for an ascent, before skiing down through glades. And using waxed or waxless skis, skiers can cover many miles of terrain in good nordic fashion. While some backcountry areas are suitable for beginners (Little River, Nebraska Notch), skiers just starting out will do well to develop confidence at a touring center on groomed trails.

Mount Mansfield Region

With a trail network of about 200 miles, several challenging mountain traverses, steep and narrow alpine-style descents, miles of mellow woods skiing, and six interconnected cross country ski touring centers, the Stowe-Underhill-Jeff area is unequalled in New England. Some of the classic trips are described below, and the map shows in a general way how the backcountry trails and ski centers interconnect.

Bolton to Trapps Trail (Catamount Trail)

This challenging tour from **Bolton Valley Ski Area** to Stowe is probably the classic backcountry ski tour in Vermont. It can be done in either direction but has less climbing and much better telemarking when starting from Bolton. After leaving the Bolton ski area, you pass through a glade of birches, contour across the face of **Bolton Mountain**, and finally descend 2,000' into Nebraska Valley. There are good views of Cottonbrook Basin and south to Camel's Hump along the way. Continue to the **Trapp Family** ski trail network via Old County Road to Russell Knoll and follow signs to the Trapp ski shop and lodge. See color plate 14.

20 km, 4–7 hours. A demanding tour in remote terrain.

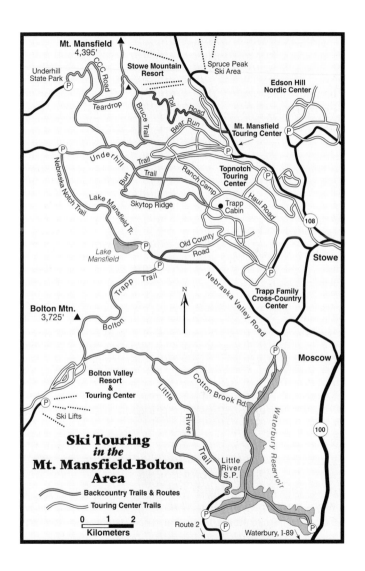

Mt. Mansfield ▲
4,395'

Underhill
State Park Ⓟ

CCC Road

**Stowe Mountain
Resort** ▲

Spruce Peak
Ski Area

**Edson Hill
Nordic Center**

Teardrop

Bruce Trail

Toll Road

Bear Run

**Mt. Mansfield
Touring Center** Ⓟ

Ⓟ

Underhill   Trail

Burt   Trail

Ranch Camp

**Topnotch
Touring
Center** Ⓟ

Lake Mansfield Tr.

Skytop Ridge

● **Trapp
Cabin**

Haul Road

Nebraska Notch Trail

*Lake
Mansfield* Ⓟ

Old County   Road

Ⓟ

108

Stowe

Trapp   Trail

Ⓟ

Nebraska Valley Road

Ⓟ

**Trapp Family
Cross-Country
Center**

Bolton Mtn. ▲
3,725'

Bolton

Ⓟ

Moscow

**Bolton Valley
Resort
&
Touring Center**

Little   River

Cotton Brook Rd.

Ⓟ

Ski Lifts

100

N
↑

Waterbury Reservoir

**Ski Touring
in the
Mt. Mansfield-Bolton
Area**

Little
River
Trail

Little
River
S.P.

∿∿ Backcountry Trails & Routes
∿∿ Touring Center Trails

0   1   2
Kilometers

Ⓟ

Route 2 →

Ⓟ

Waterbury, I-89 →

Ⓟ

Backcountry Skiing   175

Skytop and Burt Trail Loop

A favorite, this route ascends and traverses Skytop Ridge to Dewey Saddle. It offers good viewpoints from short spur trails. Traveling a unique, high place in beautiful hardwoods, the trail starts (left) from the **Haul Road**, below the **Trapp Cabin** (Slayton Pasture Cabin), just past the turnoff to Slayton Pasture. Initial steepness gradually gives way to an undulating climb. Towards the end, the trail works its way through dense balsam firs before dropping very steeply into **Dewey Saddle** and the Burt Trail. To finish the standard loop, ski down the Burt Trail (good glade skiing), and then take a right (sign; red markers) on the **Underhill Trail**, which traverses relatively easy terrain back to the Haul Road, completing the 2- to 3-hour loop.

Burt Trail

A telemarker's dream in powder, the upper section is worth the climb to get there. Up here, the hardwood forest is magnificent, and you will see some really huge white birches, trees that were too remote for loggers to bother with. The Burt drops a total of about 1,800' from **Dewey Saddle** into **Ranch Valley**, with the upper section offering about 800 to 900 feet of vertical. Most skiers access it from the **Stowe Mountain Resort Cross Country Ski Center**, located just off Route 108. (See the description above for access from Skytop Ridge and Trapps.) From the ski center (pay the trail fee), ski on groomed trails (consult the posted maps) to where the Burt Trail leaves the ski area and turns into a backcountry trail. From this point (sign), settle in for a long climb (be prepared to find it untracked) using either skins or waxed skis. After about 500 feet of climbing you will cross the **Underhill Trail**, and once you reach Dewey Saddle, you get to turn around and ski down!

Cold conditions on a circuit of Camel's Hump   J. Gange

Overland and Underhill Trails

Linking Underhill with the Trapp and Mt. Mansfield touring centers, this important route lets you ski from the Burlington side of Mansfield to Stowe. Generally of moderate difficulty (it is a traverse, basically), it does cross some very steep terrain between the Long Trail and the Burt Trail. Prevailing snow conditions can make a huge difference in the difficulty of the route. (Note: There is a designated winter parking area near Maple Valley Farm; winter users should park here. This places you about a mile from the usual summer parking at the end of Stevensville Road.)

From the **Stevensville Road** parking area, head up the hiking trail to Nebraska Notch, and after about 150 yards, veer left on the **Overland Trail**, probably unmarked. The trail climbs quite gradually at first, then moderately, as it uses switchbacks to gain altitude. During times of lean snow-cover the various stream crossings may pose a problem, especially on your descent, so bear this in mind.

Once you pass over the ridge—you will cross the Long Trail probably without noticing it—the Overland Trail branches left and descends to the Mansfield Ski Touring trail system, while the **Underhill Trail** begins a descending traverse of the very steep northern flank of Dewey Mountain. While there are no sustained, steep descents, a number of tricky places have to be negotiated, and intermediate skiers will find themselves tested no matter what the ski conditions. The terrain eases as you approach the Burt Trail, and after crossing the Burt, things get downright easy all the way to the **Haul Road** on the Trapp trail system. Bear right on the Haul Rd. about 1 km to reach the **Trapp Cabin**.

About 3-5 hours from Stevensville parking to the Trapp cabin; recommended for advanced skiers.

The Great Trail Blazer, Warren Beeken, leads the way   L. Borie

CCC Road

This route gives you a chance to see up close the imposing west side of Mount Mansfield. From the gate at **Underhill State Park** (or lower down, depending on current snow conditions), ski up the graded CCC Road for 2 miles to its end. This road is generally excellent for intermediate level skiers. 7 km. roundtrip, 2-3 hours. Moderately easy, although it can be rutted and icy. The hiking trails on Mansfield are generally much too steep and narrow to offer any skiing enjoyment. Near its upper end, the CCC Road crosses the **Teardrop Trail**, a popular ski trail which drops off the summit ridge of Mansfield near the Nose. See page 180 for a description of the Teardrop.

Maps: *Northern Vermont Nordic Ski Map (Map Adventures); Northern Vermont Biking (Map Adventures)*

Nebraska Notch Trail

From the parking area at the end of Stevensville road (snow conditions usually require parking lower down at the winter parking area), take the Nebraska Notch hiking trail up a gentle climb and across easy terrain to the beaver ponds at the base of impressive Nebraska Notch. This is a popular 4-mile round trip for beginner and intermediate skiers.

Little River State Park

A bit farther afield—it is approached from Waterbury—the Little River area (**Cotton Brook Basin**) contains a network of trails and old roads in generally moderate terrain, i.e. great nordic skiing. The large **Waterbury Reservoir** (popular with ice fishermen) offers a complete change from steep, wooded trails. The main route from the dam through to Moscow (groomed for snowmobiles) is excellent and can be combined with skiing the length of the reservoir for a great loop that takes 3 to 5 hours. Use extreme caution on the reservoir, especially near streams and along the shoreline.

Teardrop Trail (west side of Mt. Mansfield)

The area's classic ski descent plunges off Mansfield's summit ridge. Steep and very narrow at the top, the trail widens and the terrain moderates as you descend. It can be approached from above by riding the lift to the Octagon (**Stowe Mountain Resort**) and skiing up and over the summit ridge on the TV Road (continuation of the Toll Road), but most ski up the **CCC Road** to where it intersects the Teardrop, or use the Lower Teardrop from Underhill State Park. You will need climbing skins for this ascent. Easily picked out from Underhill Center, the Teardrop Trail appears as a thin white line just north of Maple Ridge. **Difficulty rating: Expert.**

Bruce Trail

Although a less serious undertaking than Teardrop, the Bruce Trail is still a challenging run requiring quick reflexes. Beginning from the Octagon (take the lift at Stowe Mountain Resort), it drops 2,000' into **Ranch Valley**, merging with the **Overland Trail** (cross country ski trail, Mt. Mansfield Touring Center) after a mile.

Beaver Meadow Trail

A little north of Stowe, the Sterling Brook–Mud City area offers some good backcountry skiing of moderate difficulty, and the **Catamount Trail** passes through the area. To do the ca. 10 km. roundtrip to **Beaver Meadow Lodge**, park at the end of Beaver Meadow Road (it branches off Mud City Loop) and follow the hiking trail to the loop trail around the meadow. Head left to reach GMC's Beaver Meadow Lodge, which is nestled at the base of the steep flank of the Sterling Range. Once you reach the loop trail, it is easy to cut through the trees to ski or snowshoe out onto the huge, open meadow. See color plate 15 for a typical winter view from the meadow.

Honey Hollow (Camel's Hump north side)

This north-facing basin is a favorite section of the **Catamount Trail**. As it is in somewhat remote terrain, and the initial part of the descent has steep, narrow sections, the tour is advanced. Usually accessed from Camel's Hump Skiers' Association trail network in Huntington, from the top of Logger's Loop ski run, the 5-mile trail descends 1,600' to the Winooski River in Jonesville. It is easier to ski up the trail and then back to your car. Park on River Rd., 2.5 miles east of the Jonesville bridge.

Catamount Ski Trail

The Catamount Trail (CT) is a 300-mile public-access, winter-use only, ski trail that runs the length of Vermont from Massachusetts to Canada. It is a cross-country ski trail that that was founded in 1984 and was fully linked together in 2008. Thousands of skiers and snowshoers take to the trail every winter season — most for the day, many on **Catamount Trail Association** (CTA) tours, and some to ski end-to-end — all enjoying the backcountry, touring center, farmland and village surroundings along the way.

The CT is characterized by great diversity, both in terms of the difficulty of the route and the remoteness of the various sections. There is something for everyone, regardless of your ability level and the time available. The CT passes through the groomed trail systems of 10 nordic ski centers and also traverses remote sections of wilderness within several Vermont State Forests and the Green Mountain National Forest. Inn to Inn skiing is available in some areas of the state. Be aware that while you may be adequately skilled and equipped for one section, you may not necessarily be so for other sections.

The CTA is a non-profit, member-driven organization that develops, manages, and conserves the CT. The CTA builds partnerships to support the Trail, and fosters awareness and stewardship of Vermont's diverse landscapes through promotion and use of the Trail. The organization also advocates backcountry and cross-country skiing and snowshoeing for the quality of life, recreational, health, economic and educational benefits they provide.

Approximately 165 miles of the 300-mile Catamount Trail cross private land (the remaining miles are located on state and federal land). These 165 miles are constantly

On the Catamount Trail, Bolton to Trapp's   Jim Fredericks

in jeopardy of closure due to development pressure and changing ownership. Since 1998, the number of landowners that host the Trail has more than doubled as a result of subdivision and sales. In response to this threat, CTA initiated a Trail Protection Program to permanently conserve the trail corridor. CTA works with willing landowners to acquire permanent trail easements across their properties by purchase and by donation. CTA also partners with the state of Vermont, the Green Mountain National Forest, and many land trusts and conservation groups on conservation projects that include the Catamount Trail within a given parcel's boundaries. To date nearly 80 miles of the Trail have been permanently conserved with easements held by CTA or a conservation partner. CTA is committed to conserving the remaining unprotected miles of the Trail.

The CTA, based in Burlington, publishes the Catamount Trail Guidebook, a complete section-by-section guide to the 300-mile trail. Learn more about the CTA, its winter tours, and other special events held throughout the year at www.catamounttrail.org.

Huntington Gap

The full version of this long tour starts from Mad River Barn (Waitsfield), ascends Phenn Basin, and crosses the main ridge of the Green Mountains, before dropping steeply out of Huntington Gap and commencing a long northerly traverse above Huntington Valley (at about 1,500'), reaching Camel's Hump Nordic Ski Center after 15 miles. A 6-mile version of the route is to bail out at the first opportunity on the Huntington side, in Hanksville. Huntington Gap can be done as an out-and-back trip by using the excellent snowmobile trail which starts at the end of Trapp Road, above Huntington Center.

Blueberry Hill to Breadloaf

A 9.5-mile ski over moderate, gently rolling terrain from **Goshen** to **Ripton**, the trail is done in either direction or as a round trip, and it is a very accessible and popular segment of the **Catamount Trail**. This ski runs from the cross country ski area at the **Blueberry Hill Inn** to the Rickert Ski Center (Breadloaf campus) on Route 125, a short distance from Middlebury. This is an excellent trail for skiers wanting to try out the backcountry. South of Blueberry Hill, the trail continues to Goshen. A variation through Leicester Hollow takes you directly to the Churchill House Inn on Route 73 in Goshen.

Somerset Reservoir

This relatively remote section of the **Catamount Trail** runs along the east shore of Somerset Reservoir, deep in the Green Mountain National Forest. From the parking on **Kelley Stand Road** (south of Stratton Mountain), the trail heads south on the access road to Grout Pond, passing the pond to the west. Continuing south, it soon reaches Somerset Reservoir and runs along its east side, reaching the dam (and access road) at the south end, for a total distance of 7.5 miles. The **Grout Pond** area has a network of ski trails, and a cabin is available for winter use.

Hazen's Notch-Jay Pass Area

Skiing through Hazen's Notch on unplowed Bailey Hazen Military Road (Route 58) has long been a favorite ski tour in the Montgomery/Jay area. After the fine and fast 500' descent from Hazen's Notch (elev. 1,800'), the trail leads to **Hazen's Notch Association** trail network. Their well-maintained trail system offers a variety of trails, including some with spectacular views of the North Country.

Selected Hikes

The following is a "must-do" list of Vermont mountain hikes. Selected for their views, interesting trails, or local significance, each hike is described in detail in the guide.

Mount Mansfield 4,395' *The Chin* is the high point of Mount Mansfield. Perhaps the most popular route is via the Long Trail from Route 108. The GMC's Taft Lodge is located below the final steep push to the open summit.

The Forehead (3,940') A secondary summit of Mansfield, climbed via Maple Ridge or the LT south (or loop using both) from Underhill Center. Maple Ridge is one of the more exciting climbs in the Northeast: great views, extensive open rock slabs.

Nebraska Notch 1,850' Approaching from the east, this moderate hike takes you past Lake Mansfield Trout Club and up past a large beaver pond to Taylor Lodge on the Long Trail.

Camel's Hump 4,083' is Vermont's iconic peak. There are 5 ways to climb it, plus many variations. Its rocky, compact summit—above the tree line—is what we want a mountaintop to be! There are no roads, no buildings and no ski area interfering with the experience. When approached from the north via the Long Trail (Bamforth Ridge), it demands 4,000 feet of climbing.

Mt. Hunger 3,538' Although not much to look at, Mt. Hunger does offer a solid hike, good vertical gain and panoramic summit views. Can be climbed from either the west (Stowe) or the east. The Skyline Trail links Hunger with Stowe Pinnacle.

Stowe Pinnacle 2,740' A very popular Stowe outing. This relatively short, but steep hike leads to an open, rocky summit with superb views of the Stowe area, and north and south along the Green Mountains.

Mt. Elmore 2,608' is an isolated northern sentinel of the Worcester Range. A state park at the base offers camping, picnicking and lake swimming. Good local views from the summit fire tower.

Whiteface Mountain 3,714' Traversed by the Long Trail, Whiteface is the prominent, steep-sided peak that appears as the northern outlier of the Mt. Mansfield group of peaks. Hike past a pristine mountain meadow to great summit views.

Belvidere Mountain 3,360' A solid hike (on the Long Trail) with plenty of vertical, Belvidere rewards you with a 70' fire tower. Terrific views of the North Country from this airy perch.

Mount Pisgah 2,751' Mt. Pisgah, together with fjord-like Lake Willoughby, is one of the scenic highlights of Vermont, and it is the classic hike of the Northeast Kingdom. The cliff top views of Lake Willoughby, 1,200 below, are among the best.

Burnt Rock Mountain 3,160' A local favorite and a connoisseur's mountain, Burnt Rock offers a solid hike to great views. The final section along the Long Trail leads up interesting slabs to the open summit.

Mount Abraham 4,006' As the lowest of Vermont's 5 4,000'-ers, Mt. Abe just barely reaches above the tree line. Panoramic views, and a favorite during Fall foliage. From Lincoln Gap, it's a relatively moderate hike, and very popular with families.

Mount Ascutney 3,150' This steep, stand-alone mountain is a prominent central Vermont landmark, and it offers far-reaching views in all directions. Four different hiking routes ascend to the viewing platform on the summit. Ascutney State Park offers camping and a paved road part way to the top.

Snake Mountain 1,287' Middlebury's best local hike, Snake Mountain offers terrific westerly views across nearby Lake Champlain to the Adirondacks. The easy to moderate trail ascends from the south to a cliff top perch.

Killington Peak 4,241' Not so much a hiker's mountain as a skier's mountain, Killington is home to the major ski area of the same name. The best hiking routes are from the north and the west. There are good views from the antenna-cluttered summit.

Mt. Baker 2,850' The ascent of Mt. Baker from the west (Dorset) is direct and steep in places and finishes on pleasant rock slabs. There are good views to the west and north. The loop south past Griffith Lake is worthwhile.

Stratton Mountain 3,936' Like Killington, Stratton is home to a major ski resort, but in this case the actual summit is separate, 0.7 mile south of the ski area. There are multistate views from the summit fire tower.

Mount Equinox 3,825' High and massive, Equinox towers over Manchester. Of the Vermont summits, none requires more vertical ascent up its regular route(s) than Equinox: 2,750'. There is however a (toll) road to the top. Good views from Lookout Rock.

Mount Philo 980' Not really a mountain with its meager elevation, Mt. Philo nevertheless does offer a steep if short (20-25 minute) climb, either on a paved road or a rough trail. This extremely popular hike has superb views over nearby Lake Champlain.

Index

Useful Organizations: Phone numbers and websites

Green Mountain Club
802-244-7037   www.greenmountainclub.org

Vermont Department of Forests, Parks and Recreation
802-241-3655   www.vtstateparks.com

Green Mountain National Forest
802-747-6700   www.fs.fed.us/r9/gmfl

Vermont Department of Tourism and Marketing
www.vermontvacation.com

Appalachian Trail Conference
304-535-6331   www.appalachiantrail.org

Vermont Youth Conservation Corps
800-639-8922   www.vycc.org

Mount Mansfield State Forest
802-479-3241

Craftsbury Outdoor Center
800-729-7751   www.craftsbury.com

Merck Forest and Farmland
802-394-7836   www.merckforest.com

Catamount Trail Association
802-864-5794   www.catamounttrail.org

Great Outdoor Recreation Page (GORP)
www.gorp.com

Adirondack Mountain Club
(New York)   www.adk.org

Appalachian Mountain Club
(New Hampshire)   www.outdoors.org

About the Author

Jared Gange has hiked and cross-country skied in New England and the Adirondacks for over 20 years. He has hiked and climbed in the Cascades, the Rockies, the Alps, Norway, Pakistan, Tibet and Nepal. He has written hiking guides for New Hampshire, Vermont and the Northeast. (Photo: Laurie Caswell Burke)

Other Titles from Huntington Graphics

Hiker's Guide to New Hampshire
200 Best Day Hikes
by Jared Gange

100 Classic Hikes of the Northeast
by Jared Gange

Take the Plunge
Explorer's Guide to the Swimming Holes of Vermont
by Dave Hajdasz

Secrets of the Notch
A Guide to Rock and Ice Climbing on Cannon Cliff
by Jon Sykes

New Hampshire
A Photographic Journey
by Robert J. Kozlow

The Water In Between
A Photographic Celebration of Lake Champlain

Huntington Graphics
P.O. Box 373
Burlington, VT 05402
www.letsclimb.com